Blogging the Right Way

Learn How to Launch a Blog and Start Making Money

Cindy Buccieri

Blogging the Right Way

Learn How to Launch a Blog and Start Making Money

ISBN: 978-0-9893129-0-5

Blue Skies Publishing
Melbourne, FL 32940

Dedication

This book is dedicated to my
wonderful husband, son and daughter.

Chris, Michael and Alyssa,
thank you for always believing in me
and giving me the opportunity to spread my wings.

I love you!

Contents

Preface

Back in 2009, I started my first blog. I designed the site, I wrote the code and I was writing great articles that I knew people would love to read. But no one came. The field of dreams mentality of build it and they will come wasn't working. No one could find my blog. So, I started to research and study and read every book I could on the topics of getting noticed on the web, making money online, and getting to the top of Google.

I remember going to the library and checking out a stack of books, sometimes 6 or 7 at a time and immersing myself into the subject to learn everything I could about it because I wasn't going to give up. Well after many months of studying, people started to show up to my website. First just a few visitors a day, then a few more and eventually my blog grew to a large following. And with this large following, I started receiving countless offers from product manufactures to promote their products by either reviewing a free product they sent me or selling advertising.

As my blog grew, I decided to start two additional blogs shortly thereafter. Maintaining one blog took a lot of time and dedication and now I added two more to the mix.

About 6 months after my three blogs were up and running, I began receiving emails from fellow bloggers and business owners asking for advice and assistance with promoting their online business. Seeing a need for my assistance, I launched CB Virtual Services in March of 2010. My goal was to provide internet marketing and blogging assistance.

Within six months of starting CB Virtual Services, it became clear that many business owners needed help designing a blog, writing blog posts and increasing traffic to their websites. I answered this need by providing one-on-one consulting, group training sessions as well as writing the blog posts and designing websites for the businesses.

With the recent upgrade to Google, businesses are realizing that if they want to stay competitive online they need to have fresh content on their websites. For this reason, I was being requested to provide more and more training and consulting. Seeing this need for blogging assistance, I decided to write “Blogging the Right Way”.

I wanted to share the secrets I learned so that others wouldn’t have to spend countless hours researching and learning what they needed to know to also have a successful online business.

I have been told that I teach things in a simple way that helps people get results. Therefore, I know you will find the information in this book helpful and provide answers to some of your questions

Happy Blogging!
Cindy Buccieri

1

Getting Started

If you are reading this book, then I know you are someone who is ready to take charge of their future and make a difference in their life as well as the lives of others – through a blog. A blog can be an extremely marketable and profitable tool if used correctly. Profiting from a blog is just a matter of grabbing the attention of an audience and then keeping them coming back.

A blog can be a place for a family to share their stories, a place for a parent to make money while working from home while caring for their children and a place for a business to provide information to solve customer's problems. The possibilities are endless!

To many, a blog is a hobby while for others it is a career. A blog can open doors to opportunities that may have never been in the realm of possibilities at its conception. That's why I love blogging and love sharing with others that having a blog can bring riches in so many ways; both monetarily and inspirationally.

Creating a blog is very easy. If you want to create a blog for fun, feel free to experiment with different applications and write about anything you want. You will get some readers when you share your content on other blogs, message boards and social networks but keep in mind that not everyone will share your interests or opinions. If you want to use your blog for business purposes, you should be careful about the content you share and make sure everything you write is relevant to your audience. You also need to define your audience in precise terms and find a way to expose these people to your content, for instance by getting your blog posts featured on other websites they read.

Blogging is a lot of fun and it can also become a very useful online marketing tool if you sell products or advertise your services online.

Just like building a home, I want to lay a firm foundation before we dive in. I want you to understand what a blog is and the essential steps necessary to having a successful blog.

What is a Blog?

A blog is a reverse chronological listing of posts or articles. This means that the newest or most recent blog posts are at the top of page. Blog posts are different than Facebook or Twitter posts as blog posts are typically a few to several paragraphs in length.

Blog posts can be entertaining, educational, or your opinion. It is common to see product reviews as blog posts. Blog posts should be written in the first person. Giving a blog post a personal slant, creates a connection with the reader and builds a relationship. Why would you want to build an online relationship with your readers? Because in the words of Bob Burg, "People do business with those that they know, like and trust."

Thus, a blog is most successful when it is kept personal. Try to include personal experiences which relates to the topic of your blog post. Stay away from the business style of writing. Write with a more personal style and use first-person narratives. Do not write any of your entries as sales letters, instead share product reviews and personal endeavors.

Additionally, almost all companies with an online presence need a blog. Consistent, intelligent blogs about issues relevant to a business' specialty positions that business as a leader in their field. Existing customers look to the blog for advice, and new customers start doing business with the company after interacting with blog posts. Some customers even post comments, telling others why the business is so great.

Even better, search engines prefer blogging business' websites over non-blogging websites. This is because search engines choose websites with up-to-date content. Since blogs are updated frequently, they boost search engine rankings.

Since blogs effectively promote businesses, the question is not whether you need a blog, but how exactly you set one up. Blogs should never be constructed as afterthoughts because poorly constructed blogs turn off customers. In fact, a poorly constructed blog screams, "I'm new, and I don't know what I'm doing!"

But before you get started blogging, there are several essential steps to successful blogging. Each of these essential steps will be thoroughly discussed in the chapters of this book.

Is Blogging Right Me?

Starting a blog is easy, but creating a successful blog is not an easy task. It takes dedication and perseverance. If logging into your blog every day and writing a post doesn't appeal to you, then blogging is not for you.

You also need to be patient. If you are creating a blog as a business or to support your business, don't expect to see a flood of traffic overnight. Typically, it can take up to six months before you will start to see an increase in your audience and traffic to your blog. So, if you looking for instant results, then blogging is not right for you.

Blogging is not a get rich quick scheme. It's hard work to maintain a blog, write consistently, interact with your audience and maintain the site. I'm not saying all of this to scare you away from blogging. I just want to lay it all out there and let you make the decision if blogging is in your future.

The authors of the website Bloginality (http://bloginality.love-productions.com) have created a blogger personality quiz. See figure 1.1 for an example then visit http://bloginality.love-productions.com to take your quiz and see what your blogging personality is.

More on Business Blogging

Every business can benefit from having a blog because it makes your message and marketing very accessible. It also allows you to inform your audience so that they feel more confident about buying from you.

Improve Visibility

A blog will improve your visibility on search engines, social networks and bookmarking websites. Larger websites with more pages tend to be able to target more keywords. This increases the likelihood that someone will find you when using a search engine. People are also more likely to share good posts. This means that their friends will find your blog when they use Facebook, Twitter or LinkedIn.

bloginality
WEBLOGGER PERSONALITY

who are you?

HOME
TEST
TYPES
LINKS
MAIL

1. Where does your energy come from?
Do you find that you are more energized after a night out with your friends, or does a night out with your friends give you a feeling of needing to regroup by some alone time? The key indicators for your energy look at the way you deal in social situations.

- prefers large groups of people, with a wide variety of friends
- Act first, and then think.
- distracted easily, without as much concentration on a single task
- very talkative and outgoing.
- as a host/hostess, always the center of the party.

This option fits me best

- prefers small intimate gatherings of close friends
- Think first, then act.
- focus well, but not as much concentration on the big picture.
- good listener and more private.
- as a host/hostess, always behind the scenes making sure things run smoothly.

This options fits me best

2. What is your attention focused on?
Information is all around us, and the way we take it in shows our outlook in life.

- conceptual and association-based learning.
- imaginative, with broad ideas of a project.
- looking towards the future.
- enjoys the changes in relationships and tasks.

This option fits me best

- observation and facts-oriented learning.
- practical, with a view of each step.
- eyes on the present.
- likes predictable relationships and tasks.

This option fits me best

3. How do you make decisions?
Your temperament is based on the way you process the information and make decisions. This particularly shows in where your values lay - in keeping the peace or following truths.

Visit http://bloginality.love-productions.com to complete this blogger personality quiz and get your results.

Figure 1.1 Bloginality Blogging Personality Quiz

Expert Status

Many people believe that only experts have the privilege to start a blog. While this certainly isn't true, it can help the perception of your business. People only want to buy from companies that are the best in their field. Having a blog will increase customer confidence about buying from you.

Potential Advantage

Do your competitors have a blog? If they do, then you need to catch up by starting your own blog. If they don't have one, then starting a blog can give you a competitive advantage. Businesses that have blogs tend to get more visitors and sales.

Broadcast Sales

Many companies mail, email and text message special sales to their customers, but you can also use your blog to do this. You can make a large broadcast about your upcoming sale. This ensures that many people hear about it.

Having a blog is essential if you have a website. This can help you gain more visitors, improve your search engine rankings and it's a great way to make yourself look like an expert. Starting a blog is incredibly easy, and the benefits make it a necessary tool.

For many people, when they think of a blog, they imagine a personal blog that has many pictures and tells plenty of life stories. However, the reality is, many blogs out there are for the purpose of building a business. Believe it or not, blogging can aid your business exponentially.

Gain a Web Presence

Especially when you're starting out, blogging is a very inexpensive endeavor. Yet, despite the low cost, blogging is an invaluable way to create a web presence for your business, especially if you utilize SEO (search engine optimization) while maintaining the quality of the blog's content.

Once you have a web presence, you'll be reaching people from all over the world and selling your products and services in your sleep.

Build Trust

Most people prefer to purchase products and services from businesses they trust. Some people will take their business only to companies they trust. Blogging is an excellent way to build and instill trust in potential customers.

To build a trustworthy image for your business, always be sincere with your blog posts. Don't lie about the capabilities of your products and services, and frequently write blog posts that are directed towards helping your customers instead of always trying to push your products.

Promote Your Product

You can use your blog to market and promote your business. The best way to go about this is by writing blog posts about problems and issues that your target audience experiences. Once you've established the problem in your blog post, write about how your product or service will solve that problem.

As you can see, blogging can do many things for your business. It can help you build a strong web presence without spending a fortune, it can help you instill trust in your customers, and it can also help you market your product or service 24/7.

Define Your Niche

A niche is a targeted product, service, or topic. You should first decide on a product, service, or topic that interests you. Choose a topic that you feel passion and enthusiastic about and something that you can write about on a daily basis.

Once you have decided on a niche or topic you have a good amount of interest in, your next step is to do some research to find out that topic's popularity in the search engines. It does not matter if your topic is popular as long as there is an audience for your topic and the topic is focused then your blog should be successful.

Anything can be considered a niche as long as it has a target audience no matter how large or how small the audience is. A blog about your state can be a niche or a blog about a city in your state can be a larger niche market. If there are people who are interested in hearing about your state or a city in your state, then you have built an audience. In any event, you have to build your blog first.

However, finding a popular search topic won't lead to a successful blog is you aren't passionate about the subject. You will quickly run out of ideas to write about and your blog .

There are a number of different ways to find out the popularity of your niche such as the Target Market Worksheet in figure 1.2. You can also download a copy at http://www.blogging therightway.com/downloads.

Target Market Worksheet

Who are my customers? ____

Economic Level:
_______ college graduates
_______ professionals
_______ management
_______ own or buying homes

Psychological: make-up (lifestyle)
_______ conservation
_______ entertain at home
_______ affluent
_______ value, convenience, and quick service

Age range: Average age______________

Sex: Male ___________ Female_______________

Income Level: Average income ___________

Buying habits:
_____ Like to save money
_____ Quality more important than cost

Where are my customers located? ________________________________

Where do they live? ________________________________

Where do they work? _______________________________

Where do they shop?_______________________________

Which social media site is best?
_____ Facebook
_____ LinkedIn
_____ Twitter
_____ Pinterest
_____ YouTube

Projected size of the market?

Total population _______________

Target groups represent ____% of the population

What are the customers needs? ________________________________

How can I meet those needs? ________________________________

Figure 1.2 Target Market Worksheet

2

Hosting and Domain Names

With any new website, the first thing you need to do is to purchase a domain name and a hosting plan. A hosting plan is similar to the file manager system you have installed on your computer. All of the files that are associated with your website are saved in folders which are located on hosting provider's server.

There are a number of different hosting companies such as GoDaddy, Hostgator and BlueHost just to name a few. I have used all three of these companies myself as well as for clients. In my opinion, all three are very comparable in price, features and functionality.

I'm sure most of you have probably heard of GoDaddy.com and know that they offer domain name registration and web hosting. I have found that most people either love GoDaddy or they dislike it. I personally have been very happy with GoDaddy. They offer 24/7 support and the file management tool is easy to use.

Want your own domain name? GoDaddy, BlueHost and HostGator will register your own .com domain name for approximately $12 per year. That's not a bad price to have your own domain name. Additionally, you can renew your domain name and monthly hosting subscription easily online.

Domain Names

A domain name is the website address people will type in or click on to go to your website. For example my website's domain name is http://www.CindyBuccieri.com. A domain name should not be something you take very lightly.

The domain name you choose should represent your business name and/or niche. It is advisable if you are a real estate agent, a speaker or if your brand is yourself, that you purchase your own name as your domain name. Some experts in the internet marketing field have also suggested that you should buy your name, your spouse's name and your children's names as well before someone else grabs them up. Domain names run between $10 to $14 per year. So for that price, you should definitely think about getting as many domain names that you like before they are taken.

Self-Hosted vs. Free Blogging Sites

Before you can start blogging, you need to decide if you want your blog to be self-hosted or hosted on a free blogging site. The two most popular free blogging sites are WordPress.com and Blogger. Furthermore, the most popular self-hosted blogging software is available for download at WordPress.org.

The main difference between these two options is that you will need to setup and pay for hosting from a hosting company such as BlueHose, GoDaddy or Host Gator.

If you choose to set up your blog on a free blogging site, you can be up and blogging within an hour. However, WordPress.com does not offer the same functionality and flexibility as its self-hosted cousin. Additionally, WordPress.com does not offer the ability to add Google AdSense coding to the site.

From a web designer perspective, I prefer the self-hosted option from WordPress.org as it gives me the freedom to design a blog to my custom specifications.

Setting up Hosting

Now let's set up your hosting at BlueHost.com.

1. Go to BlueHost (http://www.bluehost.com).

2. From the home page, click "Sign Up Now".

3. Type in the domain name you would like to have in the "I Need a Domain" field and click "Next". If you already have a domain name, enter it in the text field on the right "I Have a Domain Name" and click "Next".

4. If the domain name is available, you will be prompted to continue with the sign up process. If the domain name is not available, BlueHost will provide some alternatives.

5. Enter your account information.

6. Choose your hosting package. You will be able to choose a 12, 24 or 36 month plan.

7. Enter your billing information.

8. Click "Next"

9. You will then be asked to create a username and password.

That's all there is to it! Once your hosting plan has been setup, you will receive an email confirmation with all of the information you need to access your CPanel (Control Panel).

Hosted email address

Another reason why it's a good idea to purchase your own domain name is so that you have the ability to create a hosted or personalized email address. For example, my email address is cindy@cindybuccieri.com. This email mailbox is located on the server of the hosting company that hosts my website.

Having a hosted email address versus a free gmail or yahoo email address creates a sense of professionalism for a business as well. Additionally, you will need a hosted email address in order to setup a company page in LinkedIn.

3

Choosing a Blogging Platform

There are several blogging platforms you can use: the most popular ones are WordPress and Blogger but don't feel obligated to uses these platforms if you find another one you like best. Try different platforms if you are not sure which one you want to use.

Registering for an account is quick and easy and you should have a blog online within fifteen minutes. Familiarize yourself with the different features of your blogging platform; you should be able to change the design of your blog, its structure, check your notifications and add new elements to your blog.

Blogger.com (also known as BlogSpot) and WordPress are the two most commonly used blogging platforms today. Blogger.com was a pioneer in the blogging industry, allowing users to set up accounts and blog for free beginning in 1999. Blogger.com was purchased by Google in 2003, which enabled it to grow using Google's resources. Today, Blogger.com has an undisclosed number of millions of users blogging on their system.

WordPress began in 2003 as the successor to another (now relatively unknown) blogging system. It has since become the blog platform of choice for most blogging professionals. There are currently over two million people who are active users of WordPress.com, and there are millions of others who have downloaded various versions of the WordPress code.

Using the Blogger setup mandates that your blog be hosted on their servers. In comparison, blogs running on WordPress' platform can be hosted at WordPress.com, or the WordPress software can be downloaded and used on your choice of web hosting providers. Below are some of the key features of Blogger.com versus the two versions of WordPress setups.

Blogger.com Features

- ❖ Free hosting for up to 1 GB worth of space
- ❖ Blog content is maintained on Blogger.com web servers
- ❖ Ability to choose and customize templates (limited flexibility)
- ❖ Easy to get started; easy to use
- ❖ Upload and store image files and video files

WordPress.com Features

- ❖ Free hosting for up to 3GB worth of space

- Blog content is maintained on WordPress.com web servers

- Ability to choose and customize templates (limited flexibility)

- Easy to get started; easy to use

- Upload and store image, video, and other (limited) file formats

WordPress Self-Hosted Features

- Blog content is maintained on user's preferred web host

- Nearly unlimited ability to choose and customize templates and widgets

- Takes some technical ability to setup and configure

- Files support limited only by web server, which likely means virtually unlimited

Who Uses Which

A quick perusal of a few of the various blogs running on the Blogspot.com domain versus those that use one of the WordPress setups (accounts on WordPress.com and self-hosted blogs using WordPress software) indicates that Blogspot.com is more commonly used for people who blog about their families, pets, and other personal kinds of topics. Compared to WordPress users, Blogger.com users are typically not "professional" bloggers, although there are plenty of Common Joe bloggers who monetize their Blogspot blogs and make a living doing it.

Self-hosted WordPress blogs lean more toward professional entities. They are often more formal. Because WordPress.com is similar in its functionality to Blogger.com, blogs using WordPress.com are similar to Blogger blogs in content, naturally more casual or personal than self-hosted WordPress blogs.

Flexibility

Because WordPress is open source software, it gives experienced bloggers much more flexibility when it comes to customizing a blog. When you download and install WordPress, you have full access to the database and the PHP, CSS, and image files that make up the WordPress blogging platform. In contrast to Blogger's platform, having development access to the entire system allows users to be as creative as they want to be. This flexibility does not exist to nearly the extent with accounts that are hosted on WordPress.com. One bonus that WordPress.com does provide is the ability to host files other than simply images. MS PowerPoint files, Word (.doc) and Open Office (.odt) word processing files, and PDF files can be uploaded and stored for use on a WordPress.com account.

Although Blogger allows and encourages users of their setup to customize their blogs adding Google gadgets and changing layouts, I've found that there is a lot of guesswork involved when trying to figure out how to manipulate their XML schema, which is used to customize templates beyond adding gadgets and changing layouts. When I customize blogs hosted on Blogger's system, I often feel like I'm abstracted from their lower level setup. Some of

Blogger's XML tags are documented, but that documentation is sparse. When I'm customizing a Blogspot blog, it's as if I'm throwing my work over a wall, and then checking to see what I get back. This interface can be frustrating.

A comparison that is noteworthy between each of these blog platforms is the ability to categorize posts. Greater flexibility exists with both WordPress.com-hosted blogs and self-hosted ones using the WordPress software than with Blogger.com. Categories are created using Labels on Blogger.com blogs. This setup does not allow for sub-categories on Blogger account. Sub-categories are a natural part of both WordPress.com and self-hosted WordPress blogs.

Ease of Use

For the layman blogger, getting started with blogging on Blogger's platform is the simplest of tasks. You simply create an account, choose a template, and start writing away. The interface is very straight forward for users of Blogger. WordPress.com are similar, slightly more complicated. WordPress self-hosted blogs require a user to download the software, upload it to a server, configure database settings, and run the installation program included with the software. This process is pretty straightforward for someone with IT experience, but for most other people it is a little intimidating.

Once a blog is setup with any of these platforms, using it is simple enough regardless of which one you choose. However, of all the interfaces, Blogger.com is probably the easiest to understand and navigate.

Security and Updates

WordPress has had a history of vulnerability to hacks. To

minimize that risk, it is recommended that users of WordPress be vigilant about maintaining their sites. Specifically, WordPress blog owners hosting their own blogs are encouraged to keep up with current updates.

Blogger users can essentially allow the Blogger development team to worry about hacks. Because the blog data is kept on Blogger's servers, there is much less likelihood that Blogger sites can be hacked.

Which One's Best for Me?

If your intentions are simply to publish your information to the world without hassling with a lot of customization and continuing updates, Blogger.com is the way to go. Because most run-of-the-mill bloggers fit into this category, Blogger has the largest number (although nobody knows how many that is) of blogs in the Internet today.

If you have the resources and desire to be more sophisticated in your blogging habits, WordPress is what you should use. Accessibility to the inner workings of WordPress allows it to be used for much more than just a simple online journal.

Joomla

The advent of information technology has certainly brought with it a host of new applications and tools that are used for different purposes. It is probably the best example of what developments that have been made in technology can achieve, and there is surely no looking back, only going forward with it. Probably all aspects of our lives are already affected by this unprecedented progress and development, and there is no end in sight to it all. The good news about all of this is that the new tools and applications that are coming are being made more user-friendly than before, so that more and more people can have access to and learn it.

One leading example of the many tools that information technology has spawned is Joomla, which is an example of the latest software that allows you to create and then make updates to web pages. It allows you to do this in a most efficient and user-friendly manner. A Joomla based website allows for the easy management of its content, and is efficiently put together in an organized database. The templates that are the main controls for the overall look of the site is also easily managed, which results in a synthesis of the template and the content. Together, those two elements combine to form the entirety of the web pages.

The great thing about Joomla is that it is already proven and it is used and even supported by very competent web developers and managers. It is also very much recognized as one of the foremost Content Management System (CMS) platforms there is. Those beginners who are not yet familiar with it, and yet wants to learn how to use Joomla might want to be filled in on the basics first. That is the most important thing when trying to get started on a new tool or application, which is what Joomla is to many.

Being interested in using Joomla might stem from a variety of purposes. You might want a Joomla site as a means of launching a small or personal entrepreneurial venture, or you may be a freelance artist or writer who would like to establish your very own identity over the Internet. Joomla is the thing for you then, and even if you are already well-versed with the many intricacies of the Internet, and yet is still fairly new to the application, then how to use Joomla template is for you. It would allow you to basically become an expert in the platform, ensuring better web presence for the future.

TypePad

TypePad is an online tool which allows bloggers to create their own blogs. TypePad offers bloggers hundreds of customizable blog designs to choose from, useful widgets, ability to add pictures and videos, blog hosting and professional support. Additionally, TypePad's built in tools help you promote your site on search engines, social networking sites, and the TypePad network.

TypePad offers a 14 day free trial. If you are not happy at any time during the14 days, simply cancel and you won't be billed. TypePad offers three packages:

1. Plus package is $8.95/month and includes blog designs, professional support, your own domain name.

2. Unlimited package is $14.95/month and includes designs, professional support, your own domain name, unlimited number of blogs and ability to fully customize your design.

3. Premium package is $29.95/month and includes designs, professional support, your own domain name, unlimited number of blogs, ability to fully customize your design and priority support.

WordPress Themes

A theme is what gives your website or blog its color and layout. It controls the number of columns, the font of the title, the size of the website, and much more. By default, WordPress comes with a default theme, however there are thousands of other themes available in your dashboard or online that you can use as well if the default theme does not fit your needs.

A theme should be attractive and easy to navigate and create a positive blogging experience. However, an unattractive theme that is difficult for the visitor to find information may cause them to become frustrated and leave. Furthermore, it's best to create a blog with a plain, simple white background. Dark backgrounds can be somewhat difficult to view text. If your blog has several large image files that result in slow loading speeds, this could also detract visitors who may get tired of waiting for your blog to load.

It's important to note that it's not a good idea to use the default theme because periodically WordPress releases software updates. When these updates take place, it will also update the default theme which will overwrite anything you've changed in this theme.

Like I said above, there are thousands of free themes available online. There are also professional themes which can be purchased between $30 to $100. Below are some links you can check out to find the perfect theme for your blog or website.

There are several sites on the Internet that offer free themes. Free themes are a great way to get started with a great looking design. As your blog advances in popularity and you're able to make an income from blogging, perhaps at that time you could look into having your theme professionally designed.

Free

- WordPress.org Themes (http://www.wordpress.org/extend/themes)

Premium

- Themeforest (http://www.themeforest.net)
- StudioPress (http://www.studiopress.com)

- ❖ Premise theme (http://getpremise.com)
- ❖ Woothemes (http://www.woothemes.com)

Installing a Free Theme from WordPress.org

1. When you have selected a theme you like, the next thing you want to do is download the theme to your computer. Click "Download" and save the file to your computer

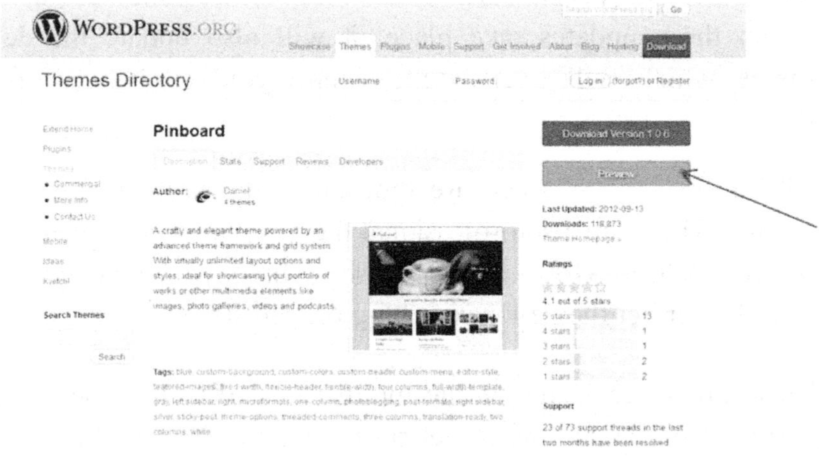

Figure 3.1 WordPress.org Theme Directory

2. Log into your WordPress Dashboard

3. From the Dashboard hover over "Appearance"

4. Click "Install Themes"

5. Click "Upload"

6. Click "Browse" and locate the theme you downloaded and saved to your computer

7. Click "Install Now"

8. Click “Activate”

Your new theme has been installed. You will see your website’s new look by clicking your website’s name located on the top left of the screen in the black bar.

Installing a Premium Theme

1. After you have selected the theme you like and have purchased it from the website, you will be directed to a page where you will download the theme and save it to your computer.

2. Log into your WordPress Dashboard

3. From the Dashboard hover over “Appearance”

4. Click “Install Themes”

5. Click “Upload”

6. Click “Browse” and locate the theme you downloaded and saved to your computer.

7. Click “Install Now”

8. Click “Activate”

The theme you installed may come with its own theme features such as color, slider and logo options. Take a moment to browse the features of your particular theme. Every theme is different as well as the features and options that come with it. If you aren’t sure how to customize a particular theme, do a quick search on Google for instructions for that theme. The look and appearance of your blog can actually have an effect on how well your blog performs with attracting new visitors and encouraging repeat visitors. When choosing a template, it’s important to think about what message you want to convey as well as what type of visitors you want to attract.

Your blog should also be easy to navigate and pleasing to the eye. If a blog has an unattractive color scheme, that could cause visitors to leave before they even had to chance to read any of your content. You have three seconds to capture the visitor's attention.

Installing WordPress Plugins

WordPress Plugins are applications that allow you to add functionality and tools to your website. There are plugins for almost any function you can image. Some of these include events calendars, shopping carts, social media applications, ad managers, photo galleries and search engine optimization aids. And the list goes on and on.

There are hundreds of plugins that are free and available on wordpress.org. Some of the more advanced plugins that include a lot of complicated programming require you to purchase a license. These can start at $30 and go up from there.

Installing plugins is relatively simple. However, configuring them can get tricky. Some plugins come with user guides or online documentation which will help you set it up. For others, you will need to search on Google for answers. Additionally, if a plugin doesn't work exactly as you would like, you do have the option of editing the code, although I recommend you leave this to an experienced programmer as one incorrect string of code can result in big problems within WordPress.

Here are the steps to installing plugins:

1. From the WordPress dashboard click on "Plugins".

2. This will show you a list of the plugins that are currently installed.

3. To install a new plugin, click "Add New".

4. Enter keyword search tools to locate the type of plugin you want to install.

5. Once the list appears, you can click on "Details" under each plugin for more information about that plugin's functionality, installation instructions and screen shots.

6. Once you've found a plugin you would like to install, click "Install" and then "yes" to confirm installation.

7. Once the files are installed, click "Activate".

8. You will now see a new menu tab on the dashboard sidebar for the plugin you just installed.

9. Click on the plugin menu tab to configure it for your website.

Customizing Your Site

Customizing your WordPress site includes selecting a color scheme, uploading your logo, adding a header image or photos for the slider. WordPress as well as some themes offer an easy way to customize these features. Some older themes do not and you may have to access the theme's code. Again, this is something that should only be done by an experienced programmer.

Appearance

The first thing you will want to do is see what kind of customization features are available through your theme.

Hover your mouse over "Appearance" and then click "Themes". Once the theme page opens click on "Customize". Along the left side of the screen you are given several choices. This is different for all themes. You may be able to add your website title, change the background color, and add a tag line.

WordPress has provided a preview to the right so you can see how your site will look before accepting these changes. Once you are satisfied with your changes, click "Save".

Also on the theme page you may see a link for "Header". If your theme does not include a photo slider, this is where you can select a static or stationary header image. When you click "Header" WordPress has provided you with the required dimensions or size for the header. However, if you don't know the measurements of your photo, you can still upload your photo and then use the WordPress cropping tool to adjust your photo to the correct size.

If you have purchased a professional theme, it will more than likely have its own settings page. These can be extremely elaborate and complex. Just review each setting page one by one and enter information and make selections that will create the look you are wanting. For some themes, this may be the place where you can upload photos for the sliders and for others options they are included in posts or pages. Every theme is set up differently. Therefore, you will need read the documentation provided.

Widgets

Widgets provide the ability to add functionality to your sidebars or footers such as calendars, page links, social media icons, advertisements, search box, and copyright information. WordPress provides an easy method to drag and drop the widget to the sidebar in the order in which you would like it to show up on your website.

Some of these widgets will correspond to the plugins you have installed as well. For many widgets, it is as simple as dragging and dropping the widget to the sidebar. However, some of the more complex widgets will require you to select options and settings.

WordPress also offers you an HTML/Text Box widget option. This allows you to write your own HTML code or text. This widget can be used to add advertisements, social media icons and code or anything that includes straight code.

If your theme does not offer widgets for the footer, for example, then information you want added to the footer will need to be added straight into the footer code. Again, be cautious when editing any website code.

Blogger Templates

- BTemplates (http://btemplates.com)
- Blogger Templates Blog (http://www.bloggertemplatesblog.com)
- Blogger Templates (http://bloggertemplates.info)

How to Add Additional Page Elements in Blogger

Free blog templates that are available for Blogger don't always have the "Add Gadget" option in the header or after blog posts. In most cases, this problem can be alleviated by modifying the code "showaddelement" within the HTML code.

Here's How to Do It

1. From the Blogger dashboard, click "Design".
2. Click "Edit HTML".
3. Click the box labeled "Expand Widget Templates".
4. Hold down the CTRL and F keys together to bring up the search or find dialog box.
5. Enter "showaddelement" and click "Next", "Find" or "ok".
6. The search features will bring up the first existence of the showaddelement code. Take a look and see which portion of the template code is attached to. For example, Header, Blog Post, Link Bar, etc.

7. Once you've found the page element where you want to add a page element, change where it reads

showaddelement='no'
to
showaddelement='yes'

8. Click "Save Template".

9. Click "Page Elements".

You should see "Add a Gadget" boxes in the portion of the template where you changed the showaddelement from "no" to "yes".

4

Content Creation

A blog isn't a blog without content. In today's Internet driven time, content is king. In fact, with the latest upgrade to Google; its Penguin edition, Google is putting more emphasis and rewarding those sites that provide quality content that is updated on a consistent basis.

However, in order to get the most benefit from your blog posts to help you get higher in the search results as well as attract readers to your site, a blog post needs to written and formatted a certain way.

Here are some points to writing great blog posts:

- Blog posts should be a minimum of 200 words. The optimal post is between 300 to 500 words. Anything over 500 may lose your reader's interest and anything less than 200 doesn't provide enough information for the search engine robots to crawl.

- Keywords need to be included in the post title, subheadings and body of the post. The optimal amount is 2 to 5%

keyword density. This is calculated by dividing the number of times the keyword shows up in the post by the number of words in the post.

- Your post needs to provide value. A post which is just an advertisement will not give you the results you are looking for.

- Include links to related articles within your web site. This is called inner linking and will keep the reader on your website longer.

- Your post needs to include a call to action at the end. Tell the reader what you want them to do such as sign up for your free offer or newsletter, follow you on Facebook or purchase a product.

- If you have signed up with Google AdSense, you can also include an ad block within your post as well as. Google AdSense is free to sign up and gives you pay per click advertisements that you can add to your website. Ads can be selected in various sizes and appearance. When a visitor to your site clicks on one of these ads, you will receive money. Some ads may only pay you a penny but others can pay a lot more.

Now, that you have the tools to create a quality blog post, the next most important thing is consistency. The first thing you need to do is determine how often you will be able to post. The more often you post, the better it will be in improving your search engine optimization and with building followers. If you decide to write a blog post once a week, readers become accustomed to seeing a new blog post from you weekly. If you get busy and don't have the time to write a post, these readers will notice.

So decide on the amount of blog posts you are able to write each week and stick to it. Additionally, WordPress has a feature which allows you to schedule your posts. So if you have time one day a week to sit down and write several posts, then you can schedule them to go "live" or post to your blog on the dates and times you specify. This is also a great feature for when you are away from the office traveling.

You will also want to make sure that these blog articles are being posted to your social networks. This is a good way to bring your Facebook, Twitter or LinkedIn followers to your blog. This can be done manually by copy and pasting your blog post URL to your social network status box or you can use automation tools such as Hootsuite or NetworkedBlogs to do this for you. These tools use your RSS (really simple syndication) feed to pull in your blog articles and post them directly to the social networks you specify. Just set it and forget it!

Coming up with blog post topics can be quite challenging as well. There are a number of different ways to generate ideas for blog post topics. You can look in magazines related to your blog for ideas, read posts by others and just ask your readers or social media followers what they are interested in learning more about. It's also a good idea to create an editorial calendar. Just start out by planning two weeks ahead and write down on a calendar (you can even use Google calendar) the topic ideas you want to write about on a certain day. This will help keep you focused.

All you have to do is start writing articles and share your content on your blog. Quality content that is well-written, original and helpful will keep people coming back to your blog. You should update your blog at least once a week if you want to build a solid presence. Be creative and apply yourself; proofread all your articles before you put them online and keep in mind that your style will improve as you practice. You do not have to limit yourself to articles; you can also share pictures, videos and podcasts on your blog.

Steps to Blogging Success

1. Update Daily

This step is a suggestion for maximum results. Updating your blog daily not only keeps your blog more interesting to readers, but it also gives your blog fresh content on a daily basis making it more appealing to search engines.

Not updating your blog on an occasional holiday or one day here and there is understandable to most, but missing days at a time or weeks is unacceptable and will most likely result in your blog being unsuccessful.

To keep your blog traffic and retain your visitor's interest it is a must to update your blog daily. You should try to update your blog every day. The best way to accomplish this is to set aside 30 minutes a day for tending to your blog and adding new entries.

It may even be wise to schedule a set time which you dedicate to your blog each day. Give yourself work hours and treat your blog as a job, what happens if you don't come to work for days or weeks…you lose money or worse you get fired! Same applies here…if you don't update your blog for days or weeks you'll lose visitors.

2. Listen to Your Audience

When using tracking applications such as Google Analytics, you should begin to see how others are finding your blog and if through search engines then which keywords are being used to find your blog. If constantly your blog is being found by 1 or more keywords then focus your blog around those keywords to make it even more powerful. When writing entry titles and entries use the keywords as often as possible while keeping the blog legible and interesting.

3. Short & Concise

Aside from the lengthy article a week for syndication and publication your blog entries should be short & concise (if you can help it). Sometimes there are exceptions to the rule and you have no choice but to blog lengthy entries, but try to avoid this as much as possible. You do not want your blog entries to become hours of reading. Visitors like to easily find information and skim through your entries. It is good to be detailed and provide useful information, but do not include useless information or run away sentences that veer away from your topic.

4. Digital Art

Try to include non-advertising graphics, pictures, photos, and art in your blog entries. Not too much. Once per post is fine. Graphics can sometimes bring your blog to life. Of course, the content of the blog is the most important aspect and you do not want to overshadow your content with graphics, but displaying graphics can add a bit of spice to the blog. Be choosy about your graphics and make sure they fit your entry topic. Additionally, you should add a description in the alt tag field with each graphic.

5. Interact With Your Visitors

Now that you have a steady stream of traffic, you should begin interacting with your visitors. Create a regular theme such as: "Monday Money Tip" or "Picture of the Week" which entices your readers to look forward to each week.

Give your readers advance notice about a product, service, or topic which you are going to review and then talk about later. If the President was scheduled to give a speech then in your blog you should state that you "will discuss the speech and give your opinion after the speech airs. Comments will be appreciated".

Try your best to find exclusive information that not many have. Do not disclose any confidential or secret information which is deemed illegal or can potentially get you into trouble, but try to get the scoop before everyone else does. Such as: If your blog was about Paris Hilton (the socialite) and you had a blog entry about "Paris Hilton Getting Married" then it would be interesting to your readers if you had a actual picture of Paris Hilton's engagement ring. Give your best effort to dig and search the internet for exclusive information and you will possibly come up with something useful. Your readers will appreciate this and they show their appreciation through word-of-mouth referrals. Imagine how many readers will tell their friends, family, and others about information they only can find at your blog.

You've created your blog and you've promoted it. So why is it that visitors don't stay longer than ten seconds? There are several things that can prolong a visitor's stay and encourage them to read through your posts. Just one of these is…

Comments - If your posts have several comments, this is very appealing to readers and actually encourages them to leave a comment themselves. Thus having posts with zero comments does exactly the opposite and can cause readers to lose interest and leave your blog. One way of alleviating this problem is to edit the text that reads "0 comments" to something different such as "please leave a comment" or simply "comments."

Visitors are like sheep and will follow what others do. In most cases, no one wants to be the first to comment. In this case, you can ask friends and colleagues to post a comment to get the ball rolling.

Frequency of Blog Posts

Regularly posting to your blog shows that your blog is being actively maintained and that new content is being added on a regular basis. Additionally, continually adding new content will ensure that the search engine spiders return frequently to crawl and index your site. In the article, "Does Blog Post Frequency Affect Traffic?" Max Miroff explains that more posts lead to more indexed pages which in turn equals more search engine visitors and more page views.

What is the best frequency of blog posting? It is recommended that you post new content every day. If that isn't possible, then every other day with a minimum of once a week. Posting frequently keeps readers interested and coming back more often.

Our daily lives may make it difficult to post daily. In this case, you can write several posts in one day and schedule them to post on different days. Thus, if you find time to write five articles on the weekend, schedule your articles to post on Monday, Tuesday and so on.

Scheduling Posts

Are you making your last minute holiday travel plans and wondering how you will be able to maintain your blog while you're away?

Not to worry. You can also use the scheduling feature in

WordPress to schedule your posts ahead of time. This is very helpful if you would like to get a jump on blogging and write a week's or months' worth of posts in one sitting. This is also helpful if you know you are going to be away on vacation or a business trip.

When you are in the "Add New Post" screen, look for the blue "Publish" button. Right above the button you will see the words "Publish immediately" and right next to it will be a blue "Edit" link.

Clicking the "Edit" link opens the areas where you can choose the month, day and time you would like your post to go "live". Once you've selected the date and time, click "ok" and then click "schedule".

And that's all there is to. Pretty simple. This is a great feature to use when you are traveling but it is also great when you just want to get a jump on your posts. Some people may only have time to sit down and write their blog posts on a Sunday afternoon. So now you can write several posts all at one time and then schedule them to post on different days of the week.

Don't let maintaining your blog posts put a damper on your holiday plan. Use the scheduling feature built right into WordPress to keep your blog active and give yourself peace of mind. In chapter 13, I will talk more about scheduling posts.

Blog Writing Check List

Writing an effective blog post involves much more than just typing words. There are several components that will take your post from being ordinary to extraordinary. I have created a checklist to help you remember all of the pieces that you need to include in your post. Figure 4.1 is an example of my blogging checklist. You can also visit http://www.bloggingtherightway.com/downloads to download your blogging checklist.

Here are a couple other things to ask yourself:

- Is my post over 200 words?
- Does my post provide value?
- Is there a call to action?

Follow these guidelines every time you write a blog post and you will be sure to have a post that engages readers as well as attracts search engine robots to your site.

Editorial Calendar

Having a high quality blog post is only part of the equation. You also need to ensure that you are blogging on a consistent basis. Additionally, setting up an editorial or content calendar is an extremely useful way to help you stay focused on your postings. Google Calendar is a great tool to use for this. You can include your social media posts and your email campaign mailings in this calendar as well.

Figure 4.2 is an example of an editorial calendar or you can visit http://www.bloggingtherightway.com/downloads for your editorial calendar.

Blog Post Check List

- ☐ Add keywords in post title
- ☐ Set your header tags (H1, H2, H3 or H4)
- ☐ Add an appropriate picture
- ☐ Add information to picture alt field
- ☐ Set appropriate bullets or numbered items
- ☐ Link keywords to another post within your blog
- ☐ Format links with titles
- ☐ Add AdSense code (if applicable)
- ☐ Add a call to action (i.e., Like on Facebook, sign up for free eBook, purchase a product)
- ☐ Select an appropriate category
- ☐ Insert keywords in the tags field
- ☐ Fill out SEO information (i.e., fields for "All in One SEO" WordPress Plug-in)

Figure 4.1 Blogging Checklist

Month:

Weekending:

	Keywords	Title	Categories	Tags	Call to Action	Post URL	Keyword Target URL
Monday							
Publish Date							
Tuesday							
Publish Date							
Wednesday							
Publish Date							
Thursday							
Publish Date							
Friday							
Publish Date							
Saturday							
Publish Date							
Sunday							
Publish Date							

Figure 4.2 Blogging Editorial Calendar

Adding Photographs

Photographs add professionalism and attractiveness to your blog and website. Just like the Kodak slogan states, "A picture is worth a 1000 words" is definitely true for websites and blogs. Although finding just the right picture to drive your message home isn't always that easy.

Two types of pictures are available on the Internet – public domain and royalty-free photographs. Public domain photographs are photographs that are available for download free of charge and free of copyright infringements. Usually the website owner will ask for credit to be posted on the site. Royalty-free photographs are purchased for a fee however the purchaser buys all of the rights to the photograph and doesn't have to pay the original owner additional royalty fees.

Public Domain Photograph Sites

- Public Domain Pictures (http://www.publicdomainpictures.net)
- Public Domain Photos (http://www.public-domain-photos.com)
- 4 Free Photos (http://www.4freephotos.com)
- Photos PD (http://www.photospd.com)
- Free Stock Photos (http://www.freestockphotos.biz)
- Photos 8 (http://www.photos8.com)
- Stock.xchng (http://www.sxc.hu)
- PD Photo (http://www.pdphoto.org)

Paid and Royalty-Free Photograph Sites

- Dreamstime (http://www.dreamstime.com)
- Pixmac (http://www.pixmac.com)
- istock photo (http://www.istockphoto.com)
- Shutterstock (http://www.shutterstock.com)
- Fotosearch (http://www.fotosearch.com)

Always Provide Contact Information

One of the important features to add to your blog is your contact information. It is understandable that many of us don't want to post our phone numbers or mailing address as this would result in our phones and mailbox being bombarded with spam. However, having a contact form or providing an email address is a necessity.

Additionally, your email address needs to be easily visible either as a tab, icon or link on your home page. I frequently want to contact fellow bloggers for guest posting or feature blogger opportunities and it is unfortunate when I cannot find their contact information. I don't feel comfortable posting my opportunities into a blog post.

Also, I am frequently contacted by companies with opportunities of free products and services. If I didn't have my contact information displayed on my home page, I may have missed out on some great offers.

If you are uncomfortable displaying your phone number on your blog, signing up a free Google Voice number can help ease your discomfort. Check out my video on Google Voice at http://www.bloggingtherightway.com/videos.

Avoid Copied Content

I know how overwhelming and tedious it is to have to sit down and come up with a blog post on a weekly basis. You know that if you want to improve your search engine optimization, you have to blog on a consistent basis (yes, I'm mentioning it again because it's such an important concept). But you also have to write original content which HAS NOT already been published on another website. Even on the Internet this is considered plagiarism and is highly frowned upon by Google. If your website is found to have copied content, your site will be flagged and your search engine ranking will drop.

Providing original, high quality content that is consistently updated is highly beneficial to improving your SEO. Consistency is just as important as creating original content. This means that if you only have time to post once week on a Monday, then you consistently post every Monday. One reason why this is important is that your readers become accustomed to seeing a new post from you every Monday. And, well, you don't want to disappoint them.

Every time I hear a client say, "someone told me there are articles online that I can copy and paste on my blog", I get all fired up. Please, please don't copy content and don't let your guest bloggers provide copied content either. If you are finding it overwhelming and frustrating to come up content, contact me and I will give you advice to help you out.

Pingbacks

Pingbacks? What the heck are pingbacks? That's what I said the first time I received an email notification that I had a pingback on one of my blog posts. Pingbacks are a nifty little tool that lets you know when another website or blog has linked to one of your blog posts.

Here's how WordPress.org describes pingbacks:

- *Person A writes a blog post on his blog.*
- *Person B posts on her own blog, linking to Person A's post. This automatically sends a pingback to Person A when both have pingback enabled blogs.*
- *Person A's blog receives the pingback notification, then* ***automatically*** *goes to Person B's post to confirm that the pingback did, in fact, originate there.*

The pingback is generally displayed on Person A's blog as simply a link to Person B's post. The next step in this process is to visit the other blog that linked to your post. You can then leave a comment and participate in the comment thread or send the blog owner an email thanking them for their interest in your post. Building online relationships with other bloggers is a great way to network. The blogging community is extremely welcoming and everyone helps each other out.

So the next time, you receive an email notification from your blogging software about a pingback, take a moment to check out where the pingback is coming from. You never know who you might meet and where it might lead to.

Keep Readers Coming Back

It's no secret that the best way to increase blog traffic is by providing interesting content. In the article "The 5 C's of Blogging What I've Learned Over 6 Years at ProBlogger", Darren Rowse explains the importance of useful blog content. Rowse states, "As I've said many times on ProBlogger over the years, if it's not enhancing someone's life in some way, the chances are, they're not going to come back again."

I'm realizing more and more everyday how true this statement is. I visit over 30 blogs daily either through blog hopping or networking and it always seems that the blogs that have interesting and helpful posts are the ones that I seem to stay on the longest and even read some of the archived posts.

Other important factors to writing effective articles and posts include writing article titles that are enticing to the reader as well as beneficial for SEO (search engine optimization). The article title should include keywords related to your post.

Secondly, keywords should also be within the first paragraphs of the article. Adding keywords within the first paragraph will ensure that they are picked up when the search engine spiders crawl your site.

If you aren't sure what the best keywords are for your topic, you can visit Google's Keyword Tool for a list of possible keyword variations. It's important to remember that you shouldn't only focus on the most popular keyword choices as these are very competitive keywords and your blog may not be able to compete with other prominent websites vying for those same keywords. For example if you have a work at home resource blog, using broad keywords such "work at home" is too competitive and will probably not drive the traffic to your site. However, expanding this keyword phrase to be more specific such as "work at home resources for moms" may result in increased blog traffic.

Whether you are a blogger professionally or even for fun, staying inspired is a necessity that will help you to keep your blog running successfully at all times. There are a few ways to stay inspired while blogging that will allow you to reach any audience you intend without feeling hassled or dry for ideas.

Discover New Trends

Research new trends and developments that are relevant to the content, products or services that you choose to blog about to get inspired and excited about posting updates and sharing news with your followers.

Share Your Life

Share photos of your life and information about you within your blog to make it more authentic and personable while giving you inspiration to continue to update it.

Explore Outside of the Blogging World

Exploring outside of the blogging world is ideal to help with gathering inspiration from the real world and various cultures around you. Go shopping, travel somewhere new or meet new people to find the inspiration you need.

Connect With Your Audience

Connecting with your audience within your blog and keeping them engaged in the content you produce will help you to feel inspired, especially when you are gaining popularity online.

Use Social Media to Gain Popularity

Use social media to keep you inspired by expanding your audience and appealing to any demographic you have in mind. The more consistently you blog and share, the more exposure you will gain overall to help with keeping inspired and motivated to continue the blog.

Blog About Your Passions

Blogging about something you are passionate about is a great way to stay inspired and to never feel as if writing or updating your blog is a hassle. Self-reflecting on your own hobbies and interests will help you to create a blog that is ideal for you.

Avoiding Blogger Burnout

At one time or another, a blogger may experience blogger burnout. Blogger burnout is the loss of interest in updating your blog or blogging altogether. This situation can happen when you spend countless hours in front of the computer creating blog posts, increasing traffic and networking. If you spend too much time on your blog and allow the rest of the things in your life to fall behind, it could result in your life becoming overwhelming and stressful.

In fact, this happened to me around the holidays. I started a new job, my house was a wreck, holiday shopping and travel plans needed to get done. It was all just too much and I ended up walking away from my blogs. I stayed away for several months. However, I needed that time to think about what I wanted in my life and how I wanted my life to be. I wanted to continue blogging but I also wanted to have a tidy, organized home. I also wanted to allow time for myself to exercise, read, spend time with my family, or do whatever I chose. So, I designed a plan for myself that would help me accomplish all the things I wanted to do each day.

The company I was working for didn't start working until 11:00am so that gave me about 3 hours in the morning to run errands, tidy up the house, exercise and work on my blogs. Having this new schedule made me much happier. Unfortunately, I've probably lost some followers during this time. However, I'll be a better blogger, wife and mother at the end of the day because I did take the time I needed to step away from the computer and take my life back.

If you want a successful blog, it does take a lot of time and work. But you can't spend every waking hour on your blog and not take some time to enjoy other things in life. Especially if you have young children, you don't want to look back at your life and regret that you missed out on enjoying your family because you were too busy. Balance. That is the word that I'm constantly telling myself these days – Balance. You don't want to get burnt out like I did and just walk away.

Top 10 Tips for New Bloggers

Here are top ten tips to blogging for new bloggers to generate consistent traffic and to find new visitors.

1. Write a minimum of five main pillar articles. An educating article intended to educate your visitors on something new can be called a pillar article. Normally, these articles should have a word count between 500 and 600 and should contain many practical techniques or tips. As the number of pillar articles in your blog increases, the chances for generating high traffic will also increase. This is one of the most important tips to blogging.

2. Write one new post daily. Show your new viewers that your site is updated frequently.

3. Use a great domain name when you make a blog.

4. Try to comment on others' blogs. Choose blogs on topics similar to yours and comment on them so that readers of

those blogs will show interest in your blog also. This is one of the most crucial tips to blogging.

5. Link and pingback to blogs with topics similar to yours in your blog. Pingback is similar to blog conversation. When you write new articles with references to others blog articles, then you can make a pingback so that their blog post will contain an abstract of your post. It is similar to you are telling another person that you wrote something on his topic in your blog. So, pingbacks are very similar to comments and attract readers.

6. Promote comments on your blog. Also, reply to the comments so that you can continue the conversation.

7. Make use of a blog carnival and present your new posts to it. A blog carnival is a blog post that summarizes many articles on the same topic from different blogs. Visit http://blogcarnival.com to learn more about it.

8. Generate blog traffic and get new visitors by submitting your blog to http://www.blogtopsites.com. You may need to copy and insert a few lines of code to your blog.

9. Share your blog posts on social media networks.

10. Keep writing pillar articles. You might get readers even without these articles, but most of them might not return to your blog. Make a habit of writing a pillar article on a weekly basis, so that you will have a collection of very good 50 pillar articles by the end of a year which will help you to generate more traffic and new visitors.

All these are very important tips to blogging that you need to apply to have a successful blog.

5

Attracting Readers

Now that your site is up and running, you've created a look that compliments your brand and you've added great content, it's time to let the world know where you are. Some marketing and promotional ideas are free but just take time to implement while others come with a fee.

Promoting Your Blog

The most important thing to a blogger is increasing the traffic to their blog and getting followers. Sometimes this seems like an impossible task. Days, weeks and even months go by without one visit to your blog. To effectively increase traffic to your blog takes a lot of dedication and patience. Here are some ways to help you start to increase traffic to your blog.

- Post often. A daily post would be great however this is not possible for many of us. Therefore, a good meaningful post 3 times a week should be adequate.

- ❖ Leave meaningful comments with a link to your blog on other blogs that are on the same niche as your blog.
- ❖ Submit your posts to Digg, StumbleUpon, Reddit, Technorati, and Delicious.
- ❖ Invite someone to be a guest blogger and better yet you could be a guest blogger on another site.
- ❖ Add your blog to niche appropriate directories.
- ❖ Respond to comments on your blog. Doing so will show your readers that you're interested and actively participate.
- ❖ Submit your site to search engines such as Google, Yahoo and Bing.
- ❖ Participate in daily blog hops.
- ❖ Join networking clubs such as
  http://www.mombloggersclub.com
  http://www.bloggymoms.com and
  http://www.twittermoms.com
  (for those fellow mommy bloggers)
- ❖ Link your website/blog to Facebook.
  - ❖Include a link to your website in the about section of your Facebook fan page.
  - ❖Add an app with a link to your blog.
  - ❖Ensure that your blog articles are posted to your fan page
  - ❖Upload photographs of your products and add a link to your blog in the description field.
- ❖ Link your website/blog to Twitter.

  - ❖Include a link to your website in the about section of your Twitter page.
  - ❖Ensure that your blog articles are posted to your Twitter page

- ❖ Link your website/blog to LinkedIn.
  - ❖Include a link to your website in your LinkedIn profile.
  - ❖Ensure that your blog articles are posted to your LinkedIn status

- ❖ Post pictures from your website/blog to Pinterest
  - ❖Include a link to your blog with each pin.
  - ❖Pin pictures directly from your blog.

- ❖ Participate in Forums
  - ❖Interact with others on forums that are related to your website niche.
  - ❖Include a link to your website in your signature.

- ❖ Create YouTube videos
  - ❖Create a video related to your website niche.
  - ❖Provide a link to your website in the description area.

- ❖ Host Webinars and Teleconferences
  - ❖Hosting webinars and teleconferences is a good way to bring awareness to you, what you do and your website.
  - ❖Use email marketing tools to capture attendees email addresses.

- ❖ Sign up with Google AdWords
  - ❖Google AdWords is a pay per click advertising service.

    - ❖Ads are located on other websites and along the side of search result pages.

- ❖ Sign up with Facebook Ads
    - ❖Facebook ads are pay per click and located on your target market's Facebook home pages.
    - ❖Ads are free to place and you are only charged when the ad is clicked.

- ❖ Advertise on niche related websites
    - ❖Contact niche related website owners to inquire about advertising rates.
    - ❖Be sure to find out information on traffic volume and number of visitors.

As you can see, there are a number of free things you can do to promote your site. This is by all means not all inclusive. But the above items are a good starting point.

Your website is a living, breathing thing. If you don't pay attention to it, it won't grow and flourish.

Host a Contest

Hosting a contest or a giveaway is another great way to increase traffic to your blog. There are many different things you can offer as the prize of your contest or giveaway. You could offer free products which you've received from doing product reviews, gift cards you've won from http://www.swagbucks.com or something incredibly valuable to a fellow blogger – a blog review.

One drawback of hosting a contest or giveaway is that many people who enter the contest have come to your blog to merely enter the contest and may not stick around and read your posts. Hopefully, some of these people will become followers and return to your blog to read your new posts.

Before beginning your contest or giveaway it's important to find out the state laws regarding contests. You should also give people enough time to enter. If your blog is fairly new and doesn't have a lot of visitors each day, then you should allow enough time to attract new followers. If possible, photograph the prize so that the readers can see that you actually have a legitimate prize.

Readers can enter the contest by adding a comment to the contest post. You could also pose a question to make things more interesting and encourage reader involvement such as "what is your least favorite household chore?". You could also offer readers additional entries into the contest if they Tweet or add a Facebook post about the contest and then add a comment stating that they did so. You could also set the entry rules to be that they have to become a follower or subscribe to RSS feeds. It's up to you.

It's a good rule of thumb to add a disclaimer that you're not responsible if the prize gets lost in the mail. A statement such as "I'm not responsible for any prize that does not arrive at its destination".

Now that you've posted your contest or giveaway, it's time to advertise. You could write a press release, submit your contest to niche appropriate contest blogs, Tweet and add a Facebook post.

Here are a few sites to get you started:

- http://www.blogcarnival.com
- http://www.prlog.com
- http://www.free-press-release.com
- http://www.prizetune.com
- http://www.contesthound.com

- http://www.contestblogger.com
- http://www.contestformoms.com
- http://www.contestalley.com

When the contest deadline has arrived, randomly (using http://www.random.org) choose a comment number as the winner. At this time, you contact the winner via email and let them know that they've won the contest and get their mailing address so that you can mail their prize (if applicable). The next thing to do is to make a post announcing the winner of the contest. Contests and giveaways are a fun and easy way to increase your followers.

Product Reviews

Writing product reviews are an excellent way to make extra money, get products and let others know your opinion about products, services and websites. Some companies will pay you to review and write your opinion about their product. Others will send you their product for your review and you'll get to keep the product for yourself or to give away in a contest. Writing product reviews is interesting and fun. Chapter 9 covers additional ways to get products for reviews and prizes. Here is a list of companies you can register with to do product reviews.

- http://www.momselect.com
- http://www.momcentral.com
- http://www.myblogspark.com
- http://www.childsplaypr.com/team_mom
- http://www.chicexecs.com
- http://www.homeschool.com/producttester/default.asp

- http://www.parenting.com/gear-article/Gear/Mom-Must-Haves/Test-Products-for-Parenting
- http://www.allyou.com/community/reality-checkers-sign-up-00400000050245/
- http://www.cybersurvey.com/redbook_panel.htm
- http://www.kraftfirsttaste.com
- http://www.socialspark.com
- http://www.business2blogger.com
- http://myinsite.generalmills.com/

Guest Blogging

A guest post is a post written by another blogger or a guest and posted on your blog. However, you could also be asked to provide a guest post on another's blog.

Guest posting is beneficial to increasing your blog traffic in several ways. Let's first look at the situation if you are the guest blogger

Being a Guest Blogger

When a blog owner contacts you and asks you to write a guest post, it is an excellent opportunity for you to grow your blog. First, when you write your post you are introducing yourself and your blog to a whole new group of readers. Second, your post will include a link back to your blog, which will help with page rank and your popularity with Google. As a result of this post, you have increased your followers, page views and hopefully page rank. Additionally, if you can post on a blog that has a higher page rank than yours, this can enhance your position with Google.

Host a Guest Blogger

The first thing that inviting someone to be a guest blogger does is creates a great relationship with a fellow blogger. One thing I have learned about blogging is that everyone helps each other. In most cases, you will not find an "everyone for themselves attitude." Another benefit of a guest blogger is that your blog will have a post of great content. Second, the guest will more than likely create a link from their site to yours. Again, this is a benefit for page rank. This link will also bring new readers to your blog. Chapter 9 shares more information on successful guest blogging.

Press Releases

Writing a press release is an additional way to promote and draw attention to your blog. Many companies use press releases to attract media attention and provide publicity for products and events. Additionally, a press release can provide journalists with basic information for writing a story. Press releases are used to announce events, promotions, awards, new products or services, and new blogs or websites.

It's never too late to write a press release and get the news out there about your blog. Here are 5 ways in which writing a press release can help increase traffic to your blog as well as let the world know that your blog exists and is full of great information.

1. **Increased Traffic** - Submitting a press release to the major PR services will result in an increase in traffic directly related to your niche. Thus, the larger the PR site, the more traffic you will receive. However, submitting your press release to a larger PR site will incur a fee. Press releases are seen by journalists and other bloggers within your niche and may send traffic your way.

2. **Incoming Links** - Incoming links for quality sites is essential to success with getting to the top of Google search results. Thus writing a press release with targeted hyperlinks can help boost your rating with search engines. However, don't add too many links in the press release. Adding one hyperlink for every 100 words is a good formula.

3. **RSS Subscribers** - Many people don't have time to actually visit a website therefore many just read what is in their RSS (Really Simple Syndicate) readers. To target this group of people, add your feed information within the press release. This will help to increase your number of subscribers.

4. **Get Noticed by Search Engines** - A press release can rank very well with major search engines such as Google. This is a great way to get your "foot in the door" so to speak. A well written, search optimized press release could potentially rank well enough to end up on the first page of the search results.

5. **Get Noticed by the Media** - Those in the media such as journalist keep up to date on the latest press releases. If your press release interests someone in the media, they may choose to become a subscriber or better yet decide to write a story about your blog. If some of you aren't sure if something like this is possible, rent the movie, "*Julie & Julia*". This movie is based on a true story about a women who wrote a blog about her journey of learning how to cook by creating all of the recipes in Julia Child's cookbook "*The Joy of Cooking*." Julie's blog caught the attention of someone in the media which then led to

interviews and eventually a book deal. — Anything is possible.

Here are some resources on how to write and submit a press release:

- ❖ Sample Press Release Format (http://blog.prleap.com/archives/sample-press-release-format)
- ❖ Press Release Writing Tips & Resources (http://service.prweb.com)
- ❖ Submit a Free Press Release (http://www.prlog.org/submit-free-press-release.html)

Entrecard

Entrecard is a free advertising network. Entrecards uses a points or credit system. Credits are used to purchase advertisements on other blogs. Additionally, bloggers can earn credits by visiting participating blogs and clicking on the Entrecard "drop" button. You can also earn credits when other people click on the Entrecard "drop" button that is displayed on your blog. And there is no limit to the amount of blogs you can "drop" on. Furthermore, you also earn credits when other bloggers buy advertisements on your blog. Blogs have different ad credit costs based on their Technorati and Google ratings.

Entrecard gives new users to the system 200 credits at sign up. To sign up, visit Entrecard.com and add your blog and a 125 x 125 pixel ad or "blog button". Then you should visit other blogs and start dropping to earn more credits to advertise with. The number of ads you can drop in a day is unlimited and up to you.

Entrecard also has a referral program in which you will receive 300 credit for each person you refer.

I definitely recommend Entrecard. I have noticed a big increase in the traffic to my blog. Additionally, the more you use Entrecard the more credits you will earn and the more ads you will be able to place thus the more increase in traffic.

6

Search Engine Optimization

It's no secret. You must have traffic to profit from blogs. There are numerous ways to build traffic. Paid advertising, free advertising, viral marketing, search engine marketing, RSS/XML feeds, and word-of-mouth. It's a good idea to add your blog's URL address in the signature of your email, forum discussions, message boards, or any other communication media. You can also submit your blog URL address to search engines and blog directories. As well as submit your RSS/XML URL feed to blog ping services like Technorati, Ping-O-Matic, and Blogdigger.

Landing on the first page of Google is the ultimate goal of most website owners. However, many owners don't realize that there is more to ranking well in search engine results that just publishing a website online. This isn't a complex process but it does require diligence and consistency. There are four basic components required in order to be highly visible in search results:

- Ensure your blog has a proper SEO structure
- Provide high quality content on a consistent basis
- Have high quality websites linking to your website
- Be active in social media

That's it!

Now, let's go over each of these.

Ensure your Blog has a Proper SEO Structure

Search engine crawlers read only the HTML of the web-page and so it must be properly optimized to guide the crawlers to the right areas and content of the website. Put the keywords in title, description and add more keywords in the keywords area. Do not forget to put designated keywords with H1 to H6 tags. Additionally, Alt Tags must be placed on the images wherever possible.

Extensive Keyword Research

SEO starts with a solid keyword research and sorting.

Keyword research for effective SEO takes a lot of patience and intelligent calculations. Above all you should be using the best possible tools to perform keyword research for a strong search engine optimization.

For example Google Keyword Tool, Google Insight and Google Suggestions. You will get the exact number of monthly searches on Google Keyword Tool. Here is what you should do then;

1. Research the keywords that match your blog's content and products.

2. Download them in an excel sheet.

3. Sort them by daily searches.

Meta Tags

Using meta tags within your HTML is another way to improve SEO for your blog. Meta tags are placed within the HTML code following the tag. Meta tags include your blog description, keywords, author information and robot instructions.

Here is an example of what the HTML will look like with the meta tags.

< meta content="Enter description of your blog" name="description" >
< meta content="keyword1,keyword2,keyword3" name="Keywords" >
< meta content="20" name="refresh" >
< meta content="index,follow" name="robots" >
< meta content="Your Name" name="author" >
< meta content="Your Name" name="generator" >

Provide High Quality Content on a Consistent Basis

As you have read several times already throughout this book, a website needs to provide great content on a regular basis. This concept is reiterated again and again as it is vital to a website's and blog's success. Providing great content means giving your readers value every time they land on your website. Give them something informative, educational, or entertaining. Doing this has two benefits. First, it consistently attracts new readers and creates a following of existing readers. Second, it attracts the search engine robots to your site. The more quality content you provide, the more likely your website will show up in the search results. Additionally, writing great content presents you as an expert in your field. And who doesn't want to be seen as an expert? **The best way to add this content is through a blog.**

The second part of this equation is that you MUST be consistent. Readers grow accustomed to reading your content via social media posts, RSS feeds or through email notifications through services such as Feedburner. So if you want to grow your readership and your customer base, provide information on a consistent basis. If you are only able to write a blog post once a week, then be sure that you post it once a week.

One last note on this, in order for this blog to benefit your website it MUST be located in the same hosting plan as your website. Having a website hosted on GoDaddy or BlueHost and your blog located at WordPress.com doesn't help your website AT ALL with improving your ranking.

SEO based content writing is the best element of a web page. Both, search engine crawlers and human beings love to read original and effective content filled with useful information. However, there has to be an efficient use of SEO content writing techniques as well. A smart and optimized content contains the right balance of the keywords used throughout the content.

1. Use two to three keywords in the whole content.
2. Start the content with the most important keyword and end it with the same keyword.

SEO for Blogging

Many of us have a blog integrated on our website. We share opinions and experiences, or use it to monetize affiliate memberships or other online advertising venues.

Did you know that search engine optimization also applies to blogs? When you apply SEO what does it do for a blog? It makes your blog pop up in the search result pages in Google, Bing or Yahoo! Interested customers will click on your link, like what they see and come directly to your site. They will find the information or product they were looking for in the first place. It is important to fulfill the expectations of the customer that followed the link created within the search results bringing them to your site with good content.

How to Write, Read And Share Your Blog Content

How do you fulfill that online view expectation? The first step is to find out what people are already looking for. This gives you the information to provide the content and answer questions your targeted online visitor is researching. The next step is to offer interesting and engaging content. Never duplicate existing online content from other sites or re-write it by only changing few words. Create unique content with your own personal touch that is worth sharing. After content creation, comes the last and very important step of making your blog post easy and worth sharing in social media. By providing value to your online visitor with valuable content and giving them the tools to share the information with others, will serve your viewers and boost your website rankings!

Secret tip: One way to create valuable blog content is to imagine your dream customer sitting in front of you. Have a personal conversation with him or her and answer those questions and get information!

This content is provided by Dagmar Gatell.

Dagmar Gatell is a SEO expert and search engine marketer since 2008. She is the founder and CEO of Search Engine International. Dagmar is one of few female search engine specialists in the internet marketing field. Her mission is to guide entrepreneurs to establish and position themselves online as the Go-To online expert authority.

You can reach Dagmar Gatell at http://dagmargatell.com or email her at seo@dagmargatell.com.

Have high quality websites linking to your website

Google wants to provide high quality resources in its search results. One of the methods Google uses to make this determination is the number of high quality websites linking to your website which is also referred to as back linking.

Basically, Google views a website with several high quality websites linking to it as being popular. Therefore, since Google wants to provide searchers with the best content, it uses this "popularity" to make determination of where a website is seen in the search results. Listed below are a few options on how to create back links.

However, a word of caution. Your search engine optimization plan must be balanced. That means you cannot create hundreds of back links but not blog on a consistent basis or be involved in social media. Furthermore, it isn't advisable to create back links from low quality websites. Both of these options will result in a reduction of PageRank and search result placement.

Directory Submission

Another great way to boost your blog traffic is to submit your blog URL or feed to blog directories. Most blog directories are free to submit your URL or feed. Some directories may require a reciprocal link or may charge a fee. However, reciprocal linking is no longer an approved SEO strategy. Read the requirements carefully, before submitted your blog to an online directory.

Social Bookmarking

It is very important to be actively involved in social bookmarking activities. Join all the major social bookmarking websites like Digg, Delicious etc. Bookmark your own articles and press releases there and invite friends to share your bookmarks.

Social bookmarking websites are very well optimized and are crawled by search engines every day. If your blog's content, link etc. is bookmarked on those sites; you can expect your website to get crawled by Google within twenty four hours as well.

Forums

As bloggers, we are always on the lookout for inexpensive and effective ways to increase our blog traffic. One way to accomplish this is by posting to forums within our niche. Becoming an active contributor to a forum not only gets your blog's name out there but also shows that you can provide great advice, interesting thoughts and added benefit. If forums readers like what they see, they may decide to visit your blog to see what else you have to offer.

It's important that you find forums which allow you to include a signature line. The signature line is where you can add the pertinent information such as your name, blog name and link to your blog. Forums that don't have a signature line may not want you to post this information within the body of your forum as it may appear to be spam. That's another thing… don't spam. Forum moderators are on the lookout for spammy posts and more than likely your post will be deleted and your membership could potentially be canceled.

When you find a forum within your niche (we'll discuss how to find one in the moment), browse through some of the latest conversations to see if there is anything that interests you. Perhaps someone is posing a question on how to do something that you have an answer to. Reply to their question with a well thought out, thorough answer and make sure that you've include your signature line. Or perhaps someone has posted about a topic which you are also interested in. Reply to that post and share your experience and again be sure to include your signature line.

The first day I posted to a forum, my page views increased by 50% for that day. This is why it's important to try and post to forums three times a week. I have about three different forums that I participate in related to each of my blogs.

How to Find Forums?

The easiest way I discovered to find forums is to perform a search in Google for your niche topic and include the word, "forum." For example, for my mom and family related blog, I entered, "mom forum." And I received a list of forums. I then choose the top three that (1) allowed me to have a signature line and (2) I felt comfortable with and appeared to be of high quality.

Okay, your task for today is to locate three forums within your niche. Then set up a schedule so that you can visit these forums at least three days a week to contribute to. Hopefully, if forum readers view you as an expert in your field or provider of useful information, they'll head over to your blog to read more.

Be Active in Social Media

With the rise in social media usage in last few years, it has become a necessity for businesses to have a social media marketing strategy in order to remain competitive.

Additionally, social media has become a large part of a web users medium for information. Therefore, social media is now part of the search engine optimization puzzle.

Social media provides blog owners with several ways to promote their blog posts, events, products and services. More information on how to use social media to market your blog is discussed in chapter 7.

Permalinks

Creating search engine optimized URLs is one of the most overlooked SEO techniques. What is a search engine optimized URL? It is a URL or website address to your pages and posts that contains keywords. I have seen this feature overlooked in WordPress. WordPress defaults to showing the page or post number ID in the URL. For example if you have written a blog post about the benefits of massage during the pregnancy and the URL of this post is http://www.mymassagesite.com/p143, this does not provide Google with the appropriate keyword phrase to bring readers to your blog.

However, this is easy to adjust within WordPress from either the blog post screen or under the settings menu tab. For optimal SEO you should set a custom permalink of /%category%/%postname%/. Additionally, you can also edit the URL within each post. This will allow you to customize each and every post so that the targeted keywords are in the URL.

To maximize your SEO you need to include keywords in as many places as possible. This includes the post title, permalink or URL, categories, tags and within the actual post of course.

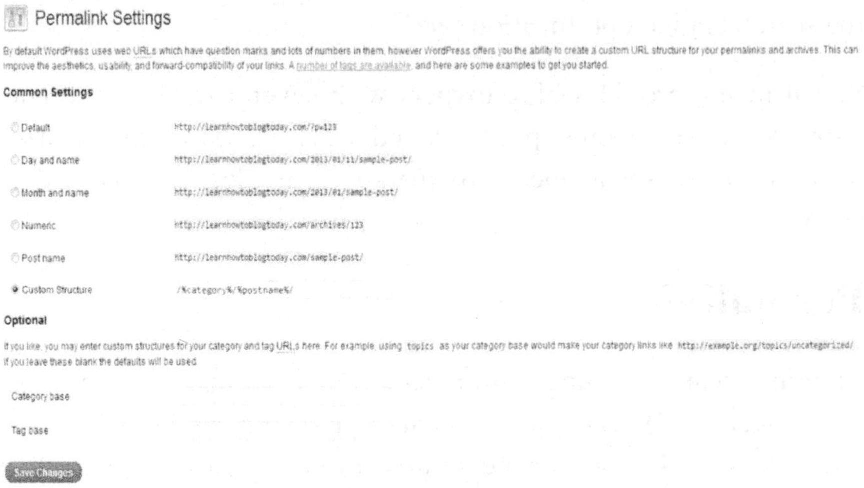

Figure 6.1 WordPress Permalink Settings Screen

XML Sitemaps

An XML sitemap is a way of organizing a website or blog, identifying the URLs and the data under each category. Utilizing an XML sitemap allows search engines to find the data faster and more efficiently.

XML-Sitemaps.com is a free XML sitemap generator which scans your blog or website and creates an XML sitemap as well as an HTML version of the sitemap which can be used to create a sitemap page within your site.

Additionally, once an XML sitemap is created, you can submit it to Google using the Webmaster Tools site. However, this process for submitting a sitemap to Google is different for a WordPress and Blogger blogs. Although, having a generated HTML version of your Blogger sitemap is also useful.

Create an XML Sitemap

1. Visit XML-Sitemaps.com and enter your blog URL in the "Starting URL" textbox.

2. Choose how often your blog is updated. This is also a request for how often you want the search engine robots to crawl your site. If you update your blog daily, then choose "Daily" from the drop down list.

3. Click "Start" to begin the process.

4. Once the sitemap has been created, you'll be redirected to a page where you can download the XML sitemap as well as the HTML version.

5. Click "Download" to download each of these to your computer.

Submitting Sitemaps to Google Webmaster Tools

1. Visit Google Webmasters Central (http://www.google.com/webmasters) and sign up to use Webmaster Tools.

2. If this is the first time you're signing up, you will be required to verify your blog.

3. Follow the verification steps.

4. To submit your sitemap, from Webmaster Tools expand the "Site Configuration" link on the left side bar and then click "Sitemaps".

5. Click "Submit a Sitemap".

6. Enter the address of your sitemap.

Check back in a few minutes to see if your sitemap was submitted successfully. If all is well, you will see a green check mark next to the sitemap address.

Internal Linking

As bloggers, we are constantly searching for ways to improve our Google ranking. This is a 1 to 10 rank that Google assigns websites based on several factors. One of those factors is the number of links to pages within your site or blog.

Daniel Scocco of Daily Blog Tips (http://www.dailyblogtips.com) explains in his post, "10 Easy Ways to Improve Internal Linking on Your Blog" how using internal links within your blog can improve your Google page rank.

Internal linking is linking to your other blog pages within your own blog. For example, when writing a new post, you can provide a link to a post written at an earlier date that provides further explanation on the topic.

Another way to add internal links is to add a popular posts section to your side bar linking to posts that readers have deemed to be most interesting or useful. Other ways to increase your internal links is by adding a site map, footer links, adding a frequently asked questions page and creating a series of posts.

As we know and are still learning, there is a science behind getting to the top of Google's search results. As we travel on this blogging journey, we pick up these little tidbits along the way to hopefully get us that much closer to the top of Google. Internal links are also useful to keep users on your blog longer.

Links in Comments

Whether through blog hops or just visiting a blog you enjoy, you are undoubtedly leaving a comment to a post and including your URL to your blog for a hopeful follow back. The next time you leave a comment, embed your URL within the comment. Doing so will increase your backlinks (links from other sites to your site) which will in turn increase your Google ranking and result in a higher position within search engines. Here is an example of the html code to create an active link in a comment box.

<a href="http://www.your-blog-url.html/">Your Blog Title< /a>

Track Your Blog

How do you know if your blog has traffic? Just because no one is leaving comments doesn't mean your blog isn't growing. Many visitors do not leave comments but they are returning visitors. I know it sounds crazy but with blogs people are more interested in what "you" have to say! Many visitors do not comment their first, second, or third time. Some do not comment at all, but are active, daily visitors.

Tracking your blog does not have to be overly sophisticated. There are simple free tracking applications such as Google Analytics, StatCounter.com, or Active Meter. You will need to install (copy/paste) the code into the html of your blog theme and start tracking your visitors. It's better to use a service which gives you advanced traffic analysis, such as keyword tracking information, referral information, and search engine information. Unique visitors and returning visitors should be standard for any page tracking service you choose.

Unraveling the Mystery of Getting to Top of Google

Sitting on the first page of Google search results is one of the ultimate goals of webmasters and bloggers. However, understanding how to get there isn't an easy task. Google keeps its analysis of determining a site's status pretty hush, hush. However, I did come across an article on Google that may shed some light on the subject.

This article states, "one key innovation was PageRank, a technology that determined the "importance" of a webpage by looking at what other pages link to it, as well as other data. Today we use more than 200 signals, including PageRank, to order websites, and we update these algorithms on a weekly basis." The article goes on to state, "today we're continually crawling the web ensuring that you can find the latest news, blogs and status updates minutes or even seconds after they're posted."

With further research I have discovered that PageRank is only one of the many factors Google uses to determine search result position. PageRank is determined based on the number of sites that link to your blog. Additionally, the quality of the sites linking to your blog also matters. If you only have three or four sites linking to your blog, then your PageRank is going to be low. However, some advisers state that we shouldn't get too hung up solely on PageRank.

We should continue our link building strategies but we should also concentrate on having a site that meets with Google basic requirements which is to provide results that are rich, unique, relevant and offer a good user experience.

Basically, the best way to get to the top of Google is to provide great SEO content, frequent posts and continue building quality incoming links.

7

Social Media Marketing

Internet marketing is a valuable tool for any blogger seeking to expand its reach. However, the internet market has changed drastically in recent years. With the creation of social media outlets like Facebook and Twitter, internet marketing has expanded beyond anyone's expectation. According to a recent CNN Money report, sixty-six percent of online Americans are using social media outlets to communicate.

Social media has changed the way consumers receive and process information. Traditional marketing was never designed to keep up with this fast-paced, everything now approach to communication. Social media has led many companies to change their marketing strategy completely. Large companies like Dell, for example, employ an entire marketing staff to monitor the company's social media presence. These social media control rooms are becoming more mainstream as companies realize the importance of reaching their customers in the new era of instant information.

Traditional internet marketing might not recognize its new cousin, social media marketing. One of the negative results of social media is that people lose interest at a much faster rate, which forces marketers to be more creative. Today, marketers create their own web pages and actively pursue consumers to "like" and "follow" their posts. It's the pied-piper effect, where companies have to constantly engage their target audience with incentives and deals that bolster enthusiasm and support. Bloggers must maintain an online presence and constantly nurture their profiles, adapting to any changes in the market. A successful social media plan is one that engages its audience at all times, providing customers with more options and opportunities than their competitors.

Why Your Blog Needs Social Media

The Internet offers plenty of excellent marketing options for blogs of all sizes. Many bloggers are taking advantage of the versatility of social media networks to reach a new audience. If you dare to take your blog into the world of social media, it will grow.

Reach a New Audience

Through Internet marketing, you can reach a new audience far outside of your local area. If you actively use social media networks, more people will notice your company and want to learn more about you. If you develop a consistent online brand, you'll become familiar to a vast number of consumers.

New Method of Communication

These tools give you a new way to talk to your customers. You can even provide personalized support to a followers through social media. If someone asks you a question on Twitter, you can instantly give them a reply without needing to use email or a phone.

Free Advertising

Social media networks provide a great way for bloggers to advertise for free. The most popular social media networks are completely free for anyone to join. After you've curated a list of followers, you'll have an easy way to let your audience know about recent blog posts or ugrades to your services or products. Your followers might even pass the news to their own friends.

Stay Updated

If you actively keep your blog involved in social media networks, you'll know about the trends your readers are following. These networks give you an easy way to see what products and services people want the most. You can use this information to change your blog to better fit the needs of your readers.

Any blogger can use social media networks for online marketing. If you're willing to regularly use these networks, your blog can find new readers.

Choosing the Right Social Media Network

There are several popular social media networks available for blog owners to use. It is important when choosing this method to market a product or service to keep in mind who the target customer base is. Facebook is one of the more popular websites and is used by people of all ages. Most people are aware of Facebook and use the social networking site on a regular basis. Myspace is also another social networking site. It is often used by a younger audience as there are many options that they offer that are not available on Facebook. Twitter is becoming more common among older users who may or may not have had social networking experience. One of the features about Twitter that many find useful is the speed in getting a quick message across.

Facebook Fan Pages

Most people have a personal Facebook page set up which allows them to communicate and interact with their friends and family. However, many blog owners are not taking advantage of this marketing tool and setting up a Facebook fan page for their blog. Having a Facebook fan page allows a blog to share posts, advertise current promotions or upcoming sales and events. Additionally, fans and followers of the blog can keep abreast of the blog's activities and add comments to the fan page.

This type of interaction creates a relationship between the followers and the blogger. Additionally, research reveals that followers are more likely to buy from a business or sales professional that they feel comfortable with and they can trust.

Facebook provides many opportunities to generate interest in a blog. By attracting fans, a blogger can have access to up to 5,000 people. A blogger can update fans on new posts, products or news and include links to the information they want to spread the word about. Additionally, a blogger can send marketing messages, offers and other lead magnets to their target market to persuade them to "like" their fan page. A blogger will then have access to their target market.

Facebook has some additional benefits that many of the other social media networking sites do not. Facebook allows users to post pictures, video, links and longer posts. Additionally, fans will be able to access a blogger's post for up to five years.

With so many powerful ways to build traffic using Facebook, marketers cannot ignore this medium of generating sales. However, attracting clients and prospects via Facebook can be quite time consuming. Fortunately, there are numerous services and tools that can automate many of the tasks that would take an undue amount of time to complete if they were all being done manually. Furthermore, Facebook is also a very inexpensive way to promote products or services. A blogger with a lot of fans will result in simple and easy promotions.

If a blogger wants to compete in today's technology driven marketplace then they have to modify their means of communication and way of doing business to accommodate social media interaction. Social media is used as a tool to stay connected with readers via the internet; knowing that the internet is a powerful tool for communication. Social media is seen as a means to maintain a sound relationship with existing customers while simultaneously reaching potential followers.

With its new timeline you have everything you need. Let's start with your blog name. At the top you got a place for your blog name to let people know who you are as well as a place for a picture to show your blog to your followers. Additionally, across the top is a cover photo. This is a great place for your logo or phrase. If you have a small business, then place a photo of your employees here. Below you can post pictures, pages, info, etc. dealing with the blog. People simply see the categories and click on them.

Now here's the best part; the actual timeline of Facebook. The timeline is exactly what it says it is. When you post to your Facebook page your followers will see it on their news feed as well as their timeline when they view the page. Need to look up something about the blog that was a while back? No problem. It's a timeline. Simply scroll back to that date and find the posting or information.

Twitter

Twitter is not just for kids who are bored. Recently, major

businesses have been utilizing Twitter as a more targeted way to keep their clients and customers updated about their products and services.

When Twitter first went online, many people didn't understand its purpose. It is a site for posting short status updates. They wondered why they would use Twitter; Facebook can do the same, plus extra. As time went on, people began noticing the personality of Twitter — the environment and the way people use it to communicate. Twitter is much more engaging, allowing users to start trends that reach mainstream media by just a simple hashtag (#) insert.

Major celebrities have trended, popular inquiries have trended and even some businesses have trended. That is why Twitter is so powerful. Using it gives you the potential to become viral.

Therefore, if you are going to use Twitter for your blog and social marketing campaign, there are some things you should learn about proper posting.

1. The tweet you send out should be casual and informative. You only get so many characters. Include all the information in one tweet. No one likes their Twitter feed blown up with 10 tweets from the same profile.

2. Make sure your customers know how to easily find your posts and post by other customers that follow you. Start your own trending hashtag words. For example, encourage customers to tweet your company and include a specific hashtag keyword that will help link their tweet to your company. Ideally, they should tweet your blog's name in the hashtag.

3. Lastly, interact with your followers. This will build community and encourage loyalty with your followers. This trust building practice will help you retain their blog.

How to Use Twitter Hashtags

Social media is one of the primary ways to reach out and gain new customers and followers. Twitter is a powerful social media marketing tool that is very useful if used properly.

Hashtags (#) are basically keywords used on Twitter with the hash symbol in front of them. This makes it possible to both link and search for the word or words being used. Hashtags must not contain any spaces and are not case sensitive. By placing the hash symbol in front of keywords, users can click on it and see virtually every public tweet with that string of keywords in it in one location.

When hashtags become popular they will appear on the side of the page for every Twitter user and get exposed to millions of different Twitter users. When selecting a hashtag for marketing purposes, keep your tag neutral in tone and don't use one that is actively being used by another organization or cause. Gain traffic to the hashtag by promoting it through other channels such as the blog, Facebook page and in email announcements or newsletters.

It's also necessary to keep the hashtag short because each tweet is limited to 140 characters total. You'll allow individuals using the tag to include their own commentary by ensuring they have adequate room to say how they feel about the topic.

TwiTip

Twitip (http://www.twitip.com) is a site created by Darren Rowse, author of ProBlogger.net, designed to help bloggers get the most out of Twitter to promote their blogs. Twitip provides bloggers with information on how to find Twitter followers, tools, general tips on using Twitter, using Twitter to promote your business, influential people that should be followed and Twitter related news.

Additionally, if you have a great tip on using Twitter, you can submit your tip to Darren for a possible addition to the site.

A beginner's guide will walk you step by step on how to effectively use Twitter to increase your blog traffic or your business.

YouTube

If you haven't started incorporating video into your blog, website or social media program, you need to make it a priority! Here are 3 reasons why you should:

- People can find you
- People will trust you
- People will like you

Videos Increase SEO (Search Engine Optimization)

You may have the best product, service or story in the world but people will never know if they cannot find you! So how do people find you? Where do people look for information when they logon to their computers? Google is the first choice but YouTube second! Second! That means millions and millions of people are searching for products, services, information and entertainment, every day, on YouTube.

If someone searches for you on YouTube who will they find? You or your competition?

Videos Inspire Trust

Building trust with your potential customer is the cornerstone to all visual advertising. People trust other people who look them in the eye and speak to them; even if it's about shoes or cleaning or charities. The viewer feels a connection and forms a bond with the person as if they are friends chatting on the front porch. That feeling is ideally transferred onto the speaker's product or service and initiates a positive action from the viewer; like purchasing the shoe or signing up for a cleaning contract or donating to the charity.

Are your customers able to "chat with you on the front porch"? Do they have that connection and trust?

People Like Videos

People will like you over the competition because they like videos. Videos are more entertaining, easier to understand and time saving. Let's face it, to most of us it is more fun to watch a movie than read a book. Sure you miss out on some of the details when you watch a movie, but if you want more you can always read the book too! And unlike reading, videos are often clearer and easier to understand because you can hear the nuances and inflections in the speaker's voice allowing you to easily discern the most important parts.

Plus the time-saving benefit is huge. Where your potential customer may not have time to dedicate his full attention to reading your post on the Benefits of Upgrading Your Security System, he may be able to listen to your video as he is doing emails or other tasks. Half attention is better than none at all and if he likes what he hears, he will look up and give you the opportunity to build trust through eye contact.

Never Underestimate the Power of YouTube

YouTube is best known as "the" place to watch a variety of different videos. More than likely YouTube will have a video on anything you're interested in including product reviews, celebrities, how to videos, music and just silly videos. But YouTube can also help promote your blog, website, product or service.

YouTube makes it extremely simple to create a channel, upload a video and share it with the public. Do not underestimate the power YouTube has at spreading the word about your site, product or service.

I created a video to promote my eBook, "Busy Mom's Ultimate Guide to Finding the Perfect Work at Home Job" and uploaded it to YouTube. Within days of this upload, the video link had been copied and embedded on several other websites. And as a result, information about my eBook was starting to spread across the net. IT WENT VIRAL!

If you have a blog, website, or business, harness the power of YouTube and create a buzz about what you have to offer.

Blog Post Versus Video Blog Post?

What's the difference? A blog post is a traditional written text posting on your website. This is the most common type of blog post. However, there is a different way to do your blog posts that has a tremendous advantage over the traditional written word. A VBlog or Video Blog post is a posting that is done with a video.

The top 4 advantages video can have for your business blogging strategy is:

1. VIDEOS ARE WHERE IT'S AT
"By 2014 over 90% of internet traffic will be video" – ImediaConnection.com. With that staggering prediction it's time to pay attention to video. People like to watch things rather than read them. Video satisfies their desire to be more entertained.

2. VIDEOS ARE FASTER THAN WRITING
The average person speaks 3 words per second. So let's say you want to write a 500 word blog post. 500 divided by 3 = 167 seconds. That's just about 3 minutes of talk time for a blog post!

3. VIDEOS APPEAL TO ALL THE SENSES
We all know the golden rule that people will buy from people they know, like and trust. With video you can create that relationship much faster. People can see you, hear you and even feel you while watching your videos. Just think about your favorite TV or Movie Character. You don't know them personally but, I bet you have a pretty strong emotion as to why you like them. You can create a great conversation with your blog readers when you talk to them through video.

4. VIDEOS ARE MASSIVE MULTI-TASKERS
Once you have your video done, you can then post your video to YouTube. Did you know that YouTube is the #2 search engine in the world? Upload your video to YouTube then you can embed the video directly from YouTube into your blog. You just doubled your exposure! YouTube is not the only game in town. There are over 100+ other online places where you can post your video for even more exposure. Imagine over 100 different places all linking back to you!

With all of these major advantages what are you waiting for? You don't need any fancy equipment to get started. A simple web camera for under $50 or even your cell phone camera will work perfectly. Forget about the tech! The most important thing to do it to get started and build momentum. In 3 minutes or less you too can have your next blog post ready!

Jessica Brace
"Your Video Marketing Coach"
http://JessicaBrace.com
My mission is inspire 100,000 women to share their story, vision & life lessons with the world via a YouTube video! Collectively our unique experiences can help change the world!

LinkedIn

LinkedIn is a great website for bloggers to make connections and boost their sales revenues. People who have a LinkedIn profile can make connections with other people in similar fields. For example, a person who owns a small business that makes baked goods could make connections with employees that work at grocery stores. This connection might eventually lead to the small business owner making a connection with someone in management at that particular grocery store so that the owner could sell even more baked goods.

LinkedIn is a great internet marketing tool. Professionals sign up with the service and list their education, work experience, and group interests on their profiles. These professionals then add people that they know to their network and an intricate chain begins to emerge. The service notifies them of people that they may want to connect with and of jobs that they might want to apply for. This is very beneficial to employers who want to retain the best talent possible because they can always be on the lookout for qualified candidates.

Bloggers can create their own public profiles. In this profile they can link their blog posts, list events, and describe what their blog is about. Additionally, your blog posts can be set up to automatically post to your Linkedin profile. This profile can be seen by thousands of people daily which not only helps the blog build a reputation but it can also increase website traffic and boost sales revenues. Bloggers should consider getting a LinkedIn profile for their blog; it is worth the investment of time and money in order to expand your reader base.

Google+

Google+ is one of the newest and most successful initiatives of Google. It is a social media marketing bonanza that is just waiting to take the lead over Facebook. Over its first year of operation, it added 250 million new users, which is the fastest initial influx of users for any SEO/social media platform.

Google+ is the first network to combine the advantages of search engine optimization and social media marketing. Perhaps the most useful aspect of the Google+ construct is that the network uses the social circles that you form inside of Google+ to affect the search engine results that a person receives.

This builds off of the initiative that was started by the Google Panda update and continued into the Google Penguin update. Both updates were implemented in order to localize search engine results and encourage businesses and online personalities to market to a more nuanced audience.

Bloggers can use the Google+ network to more easily identify circles of people who might be interested in what they have to offer. Aside from personal pages, people can also create and share social circles of like-minded individuals based around a particular topic.

Bloggers can also create their own social circles and special groups called "hangouts" based around their service. They can then wait to be found (using a pull marketing strategy) or use their Google SEO strategies and YouTube promotion to share content with people who have clearly identified that they want to receive it.

Pinterest

As social media marketing becomes a more prominent form of promoting your brand name online, Pinterest (http://www.pinterest.com) has become a viable way to drive traffic to your company website. Don't just expect to see an immediate increase in traffic to your site without putting in work, however — you need to use Pinterest the right way to see positive results.

Linking

Link the pins you add to Pinterest to your blog. When you do this, anyone who clicks on the pin will be sent to your blog. This also improves the SEO for your blog, particularly if people often click your links.

Products

Advertise specific products on Pinterest, not just your site in general. Show an image of your product on the pin, and link to a specific page on your website where people can purchase this product. You're getting free advertising for your product, and making it easy for people who see your pin to easily buy it.

Relationships

Like any social media site, Pinterest requires you to build relationships with more users to be the most successful. Follow other relevant users, and they may follow you back. The more people who follow your account, the higher the likelihood that people will repin your items and increase the amount of people who are exposed to them.

8

Build Your List

When bloggers advertise their products and services through emails, this is known as email marketing. Over time, email marketing has proven itself to be a very valuable marketing strategy to implement. This marketing tactic is a great way to increase brand awareness which lead to a boost in profit levels.

One of the reasons email marketing has become so popular is because it is very cost-efficient, especially when compared to traditional marketing techniques. When sending out traditional mail advertisements, companies have to pay postage and printing fees, however, when using email marketing tactics, these fees are eliminated.

Another advantageous reason to use email marketing is that it can reach a very large audience in a very small amount of time. With the click of a mouse, an email marketing advertisement can be sent to millions of consumers all around the globe.

If you don't take the time to build a subscriber list, you are throwing money and time away. Internet marketing is about creating an online presence that lasts. Without a list, you may make contact with several thousand people but have no way to reach them again.

Why Should You Build Your List

Building a subscriber list is one of THE most important marketing strategies you can do. This is because an email campaign can help you:

- Build relationships
- Stay on your audience's mind
- Drive direct traffic to your website
- Greater Increased followers vs. social media
- Creates a follow up system

Capturing Leads

There are a number of different techniques you can implement to capture leads and grow your subscriber list.

- Add an subscriber opt-in form to your blog
    - Ensure that the form is located at the top of the blog in the sidebar.
    - A pop-up or light box form that appears on the blog when the page has been open for a certain amount of time.

  - o Include an opt-in form or link on your about page.

- ❖ Add an opt-in form to your Facebook Fan Page

Entice Readers to Subscribe

I'm usually dumbfounded at the number of email messages I receive on a daily basis. And I know I'm not alone. We are all bombarded with an enormous number emails on a daily basis. Therefore, we tend to be cautious of who we give our email address to. For this reason, it's a recommended to provide the subscriber with something of value in order to entice them to turn over their valuable email address. Some suggested items you can offer include:

- ❖ Free Digital Products
- ❖ eBook Download
- ❖ Audio Download
- ❖ Video Download
- ❖ Daily or Weekly Tips or Inspiration
- ❖ eTraining Courses
- ❖ Newsletters
- ❖ Host a Drawing or Contest

Email Marketing Techniques

Using a few of these techniques in your email marketing campaigns will help you grow your subscriber list and ultimately increase your audience as well as sales.

Make it Easy

The best way to make your email marketing attractive to your audience is to make it simple for them to sign-up. Create a link on your blog that allows them to subscribe to your email newsletter. Allow them the option to opt-out at any time, and include a visible "unsubscribe" link in each email.

Remember that most people simply scan through their email. Keep your message short and sweet. Break it up with headings, bold lettering and bullets. Include a subject line that makes the contents of the email clear. This will draw in your reader and encourage them to read further.

Segment Your Lists

If your email list includes readers with different interests, segment them into useful categories. Target your mail to your customer's exact needs and enjoy a more effective campaign. Readers who consistently receive information that doesn't apply to their needs may unsubscribe from your newsletter or, worse yet, report is as spam.

Test Your Campaign

Send out your email marketing message to a test group before trying it out on your potential customer base. This testing will ensure that your message can be read on mobile devices. It will also ensure that your message has the desired impact.

Promoting Your Blog

Email marketing is a powerful way of building an audience for your blog. But if you're short of ideas on how to use email marketing to your advantage, then read on. These tips will reveal remarkable ways to promote your blog with this type of marketing.

Seek Permission

Don't just focus on obtaining the email addresses from all the sources you find out there. It's equally important to seek permission from your subscribers or you'll simply be spamming their mailbox and won't receive the attention you expect from your efforts.

Set Standards

Set clear expectations as to the kind of content your subscribers can expect from you. Also, tell them how often they'll hear from you. If someone's signing up for a monthly newsletter but ends up receiving an email from you every other day, he'll end up annoyed.

Keep it in Sync with your Blog

The identity of your blog should be reflected in the newsletter. This will help you with the promotion of your blog too.

Adhere to Mobile Rules

There are a number of standards that the newsletter needs to meet in order to cater to your mobile audience. Most Internet users use mobile devices to check their emails, and if your newsletter doesn't support this format, then you're losing potential readers.

Keep it Short and Simple

Make the newsletter short and to the point.

Include a Strong Call to Action

It is important to drive all the traffic from the newsletter to your blog. This happens from having a strong call to action that urges them to visit your blog and find out more.

Encourage Feedback

Get feedback from your subscribers. Doing so will help you identify the areas you are doing well and where you need to improve your marketing efforts.

Email Marketing Tools

Email marketing tools definitely take the guess work out of maintaining email mailing lists. Most applications provides sign up-forms, templates as well as reports to let you know how your mailing list is growing.

Additionally, email applications will send out automatically generated emails at scheduled intervals also known as an autoresponder. For example, you can set up a series newsletters you want to be emailed to new subscribers each being delivered a set number of days after the preceding one. This is a great feature which takes the stress out of having to remember to send new subscribers the welcome and follow up emails.

Aweber

Aweber (http://www.aweber.com) is an online email subscription management service. Aweber is one of the leading service providers that web and blog owners turn to in order to manage mailing lists and autoresponders. There is a monthly subscription fee which is based on the number of subscribers.

Constant Contact

Constant Contact (http://www.constantcontact.com) is another online email subscription management service and one of the most popular applications. There is a monthly subscription fee which is based on the number of subscribers.

Mail Chimp

Mail Chimp (http://www.mailchimp.com) is an online email subscription management services and is the choice for new bloggers or business owners who are just getting their feet wet in the email marketing arena. Mail Chimp offers a free service up to 2000 followers.

9

Marketing & Promotion

Building a blog that is successful with a high traffic rate can be difficult, but with some hard work and proven tips, it is possible for anyone to be successful with a blog. It does not matter what type of blogger you are, from independent entrepreneurs seeking to monetize their blogs to large companies looking to connect with a wider audience. Anyone can use these techniques to attract visitors new to the site and increase traffic substantially.

Find a blogging community you can join. Become an active member of a blogging community by commenting on other blogs, sending messages to the bloggers you follow, writing posts in answer to their articles and sharing links to the best articles you find. You could also establish partnerships with other bloggers and agree on featuring their articles if they will feature yours. Be friendly with other bloggers and always be genuine. Do not steal their content and offer them a reward if they help you draw attention to the products you are selling on your blog.

- **High-quality links**: When a blog has high-quality links, the blog will be regarded positively by the search engines. The higher the business's rankings, the more people will pay attention to that business and will want to interact with people working there.

- **Great exposure to a large audience**: When a guest blogger has an article that is posted on another blog, they will have the benefit of their audience reading the article as well as the audience of the blog owner. That blog has a great chance of also being shared on a much broader level and the greater the reach of the article, the better the brand awareness will be for the business that owns the blog as well as the blog writer's business.

- **Establishing a reputation as subject matter expert**: If you are posting blog articles on specific topics (whether you wrote them or someone else wrote them), you are establishing yourself as a subject matter expert. The reason that this is so important is that you want people to think of you first the next time they have a professional need that you are able to fulfill. You want to be top of mind.

More Tips for Guest Blogging

- **Always make sure that your links lead back to a good-quality website**: This is critical to your success as a blogger. The chances are very high that your readers will click on the link that you provide in your blog article. Basically, it is important that both ends be of the highest quality. In other words, the quality of your blog writing must be excellent and the website that is linked to your blog content must also be excellent. It is important to remember that there are two reputations on the line at all times; yours as the writer and the blog owner's reputation as well.

- **Be careful where you post**: It is very important that you get involved with the blog for a while in some capacity before you actually become a guest blogger. You should develop a relationship with the business owner before you approach him or her about becoming a guest blogger. Your connection to that business should be solid and genuine.

- **Get to know what the business and the business owner represents before you guest blog**: The term "guilt by association" really applies in this situation. If you have gotten to know a particular business well, you will be able to determine whether you are a good fit for that business. It makes no sense to blindly submit blogs that you are hoping will be posted. There has to be a relevant connection between what you are writing and what they are selling.

- **Sell your blog idea to the best of your ability**: When you are discussing your idea for a blog article to a particular business, it is very important for you to give the blog owner an opportunity to get to know you to a point, whether that is through Email, on the phone or in person. There are some questions that the blog owner may ask you and you should be prepared with the answers. They are:

    - Why do you want to guest blog for that specific blog?

    - What is the subject of the blog article and why would it benefit that particular blog?

- Are you flexible about revising your blog article to suit the blog owner?

On the part of the blog owner, it is perfectly appropriate to request that he or she respond to you and let you know whether he or she has decided to publish your blog article. There is no reason why the blog owner shouldn't at least read your article, even if it never gets published.

Promote your blog article through social media channels: Once your article is posted on the other person's blog, you should share it with all of your online connections, including social media groups and business directories, if appropriate.

You should consider guest blogging. It is a great way to gain additional exposure and boost your professional reputation to great heights. Of course, you should also have your own blog and it is beneficial to have other people contribute to your blog as well. So, go out and find guest blogging opportunities. Your content should be focused on your niche and your target audience will reach out and interact with you.

Create Shareable Content

One fast way to increase traffic to your blog is to create content that your audience is likely to share with others. Create a strategy to target an audience that is likely to share your work widely and provide calls to action that encourages them to share with the people that they know. Some types of content are more popular than others on the internet, so keep this in mind when planning your strategy. If you can reach the people most likely to enjoy your content and share it with others, you will improve your chances of reaching a wider audience and increasing your traffic numbers.

Use Proven SEO Techniques

As outlined in chapter 6, using SEO techniques for the creation of your content will increase your rankings in the search engines, making it more likely that someone interested in the type of content on your blog will see your link and decide to visit your site. There are billions of searches a day, providing you with a massive opportunity to increase traffic. A high percentage of the business side of blogging, including advertising and guest posting opportunities, come from searches that result in your blog being found by interested parties.

So in a nutshell, write great content that provides value and readers will return to your site again and again.

Provide RSS Feeds and Email Updates

Providing RSS feeds and email updates keeps readers abreast of recent content. Feedburner (http://www.feedburner.com) makes creating RSS feeds and email update links simple.

Create Feed

1. Visit Feedburner.com
2. If you don't already have a Google account, create one at this time.
3. On Feedburner's main page, enter your blog address in the text box below the content that reads, "**Burn a feed right this instant.** Type your blog or feed address here:" and click "next".
4. You will then be sent to a confirmation page where you will see your newly generated feed address.

Look up RSS Feed Address

1. To view your feed address, visit Feedburner.com and choose the feed title.

2. Click on the top left "Edit Feed Details."

3. You will then see "original feed" and "feed address". Either one of these address can be used as your RSS feed.

Create Feedburner Email Updates

1. Visit Feedburner.com and log into your account

2. Click on the feed title you want to create email updates for

3. Click the top tab "Publicize."

4. Click "Email Subscriptions."

5. Copy and paste the code provided into your blog design.

Entrecard

As previously discussed in chapter 5, Entrecard (http://www. entrecard.com) is a free banner network which allows you to promote your website or blog on over 40,000 websites. Entrecard is a useful way to network your website and increase traffic. Entrecard uses a credit system in which you earn credits when you visit other blogs within the network and click "drop" on their Entrecard currently advertised ad. you can earn credits by dropping on other blogs and when others "drop" on your site. Credits are then used to create ads. You then choose which website you want to place your ad. Websites have different ad credit costs based on their Technorati and Google ratings.

Additionally, Entrecard will give you 200 credits when you first sign up. To sign up, visit Entrecard.com and add your website and a 125 x 125 ad or blog button. Then you should visit other blogs and start dropping to earn more credits to advertise with. The number of ads you can drop in a day is unlimited and up to you.

Entrecard also has a referral program in which you will receive 300 credit for each person you refer.

Adgitize

Adgitize (http://www.adgitize.com) is site in which bloggers can place pay per click ads on their blogs as well as sign up to advertise their blog. Advertising costs $14 per month and is payable through Paypal.

It's free to sign up to be a publisher and place ads on your blog. Bloggers receive points when they regularly add new content or write new articles, by the number of page views and if anyone clicks on one of the ads. Bloggers also receive points when visitors click on ads placed on their own blogs or adgitize ads on other blogs. At the end of the month, the points are converted to cash. Adgitize takes your total points divided by the total points earned by all members. Then that percentage is multiplied by the amount of money placed into the system available for the members. You are then paid that amount once a month. Bloggers are paid on the 20th of the month after earnings from the previous months reach $10 to $50 or more.

Adgitize also has an affiliate program. Affiliates are paid $5 for each new full month ad that is bought. Bloggers will then continue to earn $1 monthly commission for every advertiser that is brought into the network.

Google Adwords

As mentioned throughout this book, increasing blog traffic and attracting visitors doesn't happen overnight. Therefore, an alternative to quickly bringing visitors to your blog is through the use of Google Adwords. As discussed in chapter 11, Adwords is a pay-per-click (PPC), cost-per-thousand-impressions or cost-per-mille (CPM) site-targeted advertising of text, banner, and rich-media ads.

Your ad is displaced on the right side of the Google search results page and on websites that participate in the AdSense program. To get started, you input your maximum daily budget, create your ad, and select targeted keywords. To learn more about Google Adwords and to create your ad visit, http://www.google.com/adwords.

Facebook Ads

Facebook also offers a pay-per-click (PPC) advertising program. Facebook allows you to set the demographics of your target market. The demographics include sex, age, location, relationship status, education, interests and hobbies. You can also specify if you want the Facebook user to go to your Facebook Fan Page or a different website such as your blog. Once you have selected the demographics, your ad is shown on the news feed or home page of those people who meet your demographics.

Facebook allows you to set a daily or lifetime budget. This is a great feature because once you have reached your lifetime budget your ad no longer shows and you won't be charged. For example, if you set your lifetime budget to $500, once you have reached that budget by Facebook users clicking on your ad, your ad will no longer show. To learn more about Facebook Ads and get started, visit https://www.facebook.com/advertising.

Products for Giveaways

Hosting a giveaway is a great way to increase traffic to your blog. Additionally, a giveaway can be fun for you as well as the visitors. Products for these giveaways can come from a variety of different sources.

1. Placing a "PR Welcome" or "PR Friendly" text or page on your blog is one way to attract companies. Companies are on the lookout for blogs that are interested in hosting a giveaway or reviewing their products. In my personal experience, I have been contacted on several occasions from companies such as CSN Stores and Kidtoons to host a giveaway or write a product review. You can also see which companies other blogs are hosting a giveaway for and contact that company directly to let them know that you're interested in working with them.

2. If you use Swagbucks (http://www.swagbucks.com) as often as I do, you can earn points which can then be redeemed as gift cards and products. Then you could giveaway an Amazon.com gift card earned from your Swagbucks.

3. Signing up websites to do product reviews is another way to get products for giveaways. Many times in lieu of money, these sites will give you the product for the review plus an additional one that you use for the giveaway.

4. If you can buy a gift card or a product at a great discount, this could be a small investment in order to drive traffic to your blog. For example, Restaurant.com offers monthly deals on their gift cards and certificates. Sometimes you

can get a $25 gift card for $2. $2 is a pretty good price to pay for advertising, in my opinion.

Another great product you can offer for a giveaway is a feature article or 1 month of advertising on your blog. In some cases, this may not be the right product for your blog's niche. But if you're just starting out and participate in blog hops, chances are the majority of visitors are fellow blog owners. This type of prize is beneficial to you and the winner because more than likely the winner will post on their blog that they won and will refer visitors to your site to read their feature article.

10

Affiliate Marketing

When I starting blogging in 2009, affiliate marketing peaked my interest. I learned as much as possible on it and the best way to use it to monetize my blog. Since that time, I have earned commissions from several different types of affiliate programs. In fact I still earn commissions from blog posts that I wrote over 4 years ago. Blogging is my passion and I really enjoy researching different affiliate programs and sharing with my readers my reviews and opinions on different products.

Affiliate marketing provides an excellent way to create a stream of revenue. There are some professional affiliate marketers such as John Chow and Rosalind Gardner who use affiliate marketing to create 6 figure incomes. But this is not a get rich quick scheme. Becoming a successful affiliate marketer requires planning, consistency and dedication. And in this chapter, I will share with you the steps that are required to be successful.

An affiliate marketer is someone who has formed a partnership with an online merchant in which the affiliate earns a commission for referring sales or leads to the merchant's online store.

For example you can sign up to be an affiliate for online merchants such as Amazon.com, Toys R Us, Restaurant.com or Constant Contact.

Additionally, you can also register to be a vendor and have other affiliate marketers sell your products including digital products such as eBooks and training programs.

As an affiliate marketer, you will receive a commission selling on the internet. Commission may be based on a purchase amount called a pay per sale, it could be based on a set value for each visit or a pay per click, or based on an action such as a registration or download called a pay per lead. I prefer pay per click programs and I have earned commissions from well written product reviews.

So here is how affiliate marketing works...

1. You join an affiliate program and are given a unique affiliate identification and access to your special links.

2. You place your affiliate links on your web site or in your newsletter, or social media page.

3. A visitor on your site clicks the link and buys a product, service or fills out a form at the merchant's site.

4. You earn a commission for sales or leads generated through your links.

While those are the basic steps, here are the steps to building a successful affiliate business:

First, you need to have a website that is full of rich content.

Second, you want to find merchants with affiliate programs that are related to or relevant to your site's niche or focus of your website. For example, if your website provides advice on how to start a business, you typically wouldn't market products from the Toys R Us affiliate program.

Third, write reviews about these affiliate products and services.

Fourth, market your site to bring in and attract visitors.

I cannot stress enough how important and vital it is to write reviews and blog posts about the products or services you want to earn a commission for. Just adding a picture of the product or a sales banner of the product to your website will not generate as much commission as you would like.

Now, Let's review some of the major affiliate programs out there.

One of the most popular affiliate programs is Google AdSense (http://www.google.com/adsense). Google AdSense is a pay per click program where you are essentially paid a set amount each time one of your website visitors clicks on your affiliate link and lands on the merchant's site. When you enroll in Google AdSense, you can run image, text or video ads on your site. These ads generate revenue on either a pay per click or per thousand impressions basis. Google AdSense is free to sign up. But a word of caution... It's not a good idea to clutter your website with a ton of these ads. This will detract from the quality of your site as well as drive away visitors. Add just a couple of ads that are not too intrusive or annoying to your site visitor.

Another great feature of Google AdSense is that the ads placed on your website show ads that are relevant to the content on that page. For example, if you have written a blog post on the top 5 vacation spring break destinations, Google will display travel related ads such as hotels, car rentals and travel related resources. I recommend using strictly the image ads. The reason is because to your website visitors these ads look like they could be sponsored advertisers or merchants who are paying you to advertise on your site. Sites that sell advertising space generate a substantial amount of traffic to their sites so showing image ads give your site a bigger presence to visitors.

I remember the first day I added Google AdSense to my site. On my very first day, I earned a quarter. You may be thinking, "A quarter. You got excited about earning a quarter." And yes, I did. That was a quarter I didn't have and it showed me the revenue earning potential available. In fact, Darren Rowse, author of problogger.net, states that out of all of his revenue streams, Google AdSense generates the most money for him and he earns a 6 figure income as a professional blogger, author and speaker.

If you are new to affiliate marketing, a good place to start is with affiliate networks. An affiliate network acts as a third party and functions as the middleman between merchants and affiliates. Merchants use affiliate networks to list their products and the details of their affiliate programs. An affiliate can apply to those they are interested in and qualify for.

Joining an affiliate network is free for affiliates, and the process is fairly simple as the merchants are organized by category. Additionally affiliate networks tend to offer higher quality programs. So if you have a business related site, you can search through the business category of affiliate programs for the products or services that will give your site visitors a value.

Commission Junction (http://www.cj.com) is one of the most popular affiliate networks with companies like Coupons.com and Toys R Us. Once you select the company you would like to join, commission junction will review your site and let you know if you have been approved. The Commission Junction website has all of the available banners and links for each company as well as the commission you will receive per sale or lead. Additionally, you will receive a check from Commission Junction when your commission reaches a certain amount. And that is typical of most affiliate networks.

LinkShare (http://www.linkShare.com) works just like Commission Junction. Some of the companies associated with Linkshare are 1-800-Flowers, iTunes, and South Beach Diet. Banners and text links are also available.

Amazon.com Associates program allows website owners to advertise Amazon products on their blog or website and earn a commission. Signing up is quick and easy. Amazon offers many different types of banners, widgets and astores. An astore is where you can add several products and create a small store on your website. Many of my clients as well as myself will typically sell books from amazon. To increase your chances of selling these books, you need to write a review about the book. Share what you liked, what you didn't like and how much the book costs and of course include your affiliate link.

Share a Sale (http://www.Shareasale.com) is an affiliate network which manages affiliates such as smaller online stores. Signing up with Share a Sale is also very easy and sometimes you will get instant affiliate approval.

Clickbank (http://www.Clickbank.com) is the top affiliate networks for digital products such as ebooks. A website owner can simply sign up and then visit the marketplace to select the digital products they want to advertise on their blog or website. Some digital products offer a 50% commission.

Now, you have a website setup full of great content. You've selected and signed up for affiliate merchants, now it's time to start advertising and promoting these products.

Like I mentioned earlier, this is not a get rich quick scheme. The secret is to have great site content.

I always give the product or service added value by writing a product review. I tell my visitors exactly why I think it's a good product or services. If it has a few drawbacks, but I still think it's a good buy, I will them that too. I give my readers enough information about the product to help them decide whether or not it is right for them.

As much as possible, I buy the product so I can give it an adequate review. You can use your affiliate link so that you can receive the product at a discounted rate. In some cases, you may be able to contact the vendor and ask for a trial of the product.

If you don't have time to write the reviews, not to worry. You can hire a ghost writer to write the review for you. The ghost writer will provide the majority or the meat of the review. Then you can add a few sentences to the post to bring in your personality and your opinions good and bad about the product. Always, always make sure to add a call to action at the end of your review. This call to action will say something like "click here to buy the secrets to blogging eBook". And include your affiliate link. If you are looking for a ghost writer, my company CB Virtual Services (http://www.cbvirtualservices.com) can write the reviews and blog posts for you.

In this chapter, I have covered the steps to getting started with affiliate marketing which are:

- You need to have a website that is full of rich content.

- Sign up with an affiliate program
- Write reviews about these affiliate products and services.
- And finally market your site to bring in and attract visitors.

Marketing Your Affiliate Products

1. You need have sound SEO or search engine optimization strategies in place.
2. Add your website URL to your email signature block.
3. Advertise on relevant online magazines or e-zines.
4. Issue a press release.
5. Participate in online groups and forums.
6. Add social bookmarking to your blog or website. This will allow visitors to save and share your content.
7. Get involved in social media such as Facebook, Twitter, LinkedIn and YouTube. Make a video of the affiliate products, upload it to YouTube and then share the video on Facebook, Twitter and LinkedIn.
8. Pay Per Click and banner advertising

Blogsvertise

Blogsvertise (http://www.blogsvertise.com) is a website which offers bloggers a way to earn extra income by posting articles about an advertisers website. Bloggers can write about whatever they want as long as their post includes the required links. The post can be a review of the advertiser's website, positive or negative, or talk about how the products relate to your daily life.

Blogsvertise will notify bloggers when an opportunity is available. They will inform the blogger about who and what to write about. After the post is approved, the blogger is paid through Paypal. The only requirement is that you must have a blog.

Payments range between $4 – $25 per entry. Most will fall into the $5-15 range. Payout Rates will vary and are frequently based on popularity/traffic of blog as measured by independent third parties. Payments are made 30 days after your assigned task has been approved.

In addition, bloggers can use Blogsvertise to have a review written about their own blog.

Affiliate marketing is a way to make money by referring visitors or customers to a business's website. A blogger can earn a commission if a visitor simply subscribes to the site or if they make a purchase. Commission can either be a percentage of the sale or a flat fee. Most businesses belong to an affiliate network company which serves as the middle man and handles all of the transactions including making sure you get paid.

11

Making Money

If you are looking for some effective ways to make money online, blogging is the perfect solution. However, before you begin to blog, you need to know about the five top ways to maximize your earnings. These five methods will work great with any type of blog, no matter what the subject may be.

Once your blog has gained some real momentum and your blog traffic is increasing then it is time to start thinking about turning your traffic into profit. You should use contextual advertising, like Google AdSense or Chitika. Contextual advertising is usually text links which use the content of your blog to publish targeted ads on your blog. The payout is usually based on a pay-per-click model, meaning for every click an ad receives you are paid a small percentage of the profits. In addition to contextual advertising it is good to also use graphical advertising such as: BlogAds.com, Amazon.com, MammaMedia, or General Sponsored Advertising.

Promote Your Own Product

Use your blog to promote your products and services. This can be most anything you wish to sell online or through the mail including eBooks, reports, services, training programs, crafts or other items. See more information on creating an eBook later in this chapter.

Promote Someone Else's Product

Another great way to make money blogging is to promote someone else's products, services or website. This is known as affiliate marketing as we've already discussed in chapter 10. There are many businesses that are willing to pay people to write promotional blogs or reviews for them.

Pay-Per-Click Ads

You can also make quite a bit of money when you place pay-per-click ads on your blog such as Google AdSense advertisements. When people read your blog, you will get paid for each ad they click on. This method is very popular and has been known to generate a lot of money for bloggers.

Chitika

Chitika is somewhat similar to Google AdSense ads, except they do not have any text. They are simply pictures that visitors to your blog can click on. Again, each time someone clicks on these ads, you will get paid.

Email Marketing

By requesting visitor's email addresses and building a strong following, you can market to these visitors at a later date. This can be a great way to sell your products and/or services to an audience that is interested in what you have to offer. This was covered in great detail in chapter 8.

Banner Advertisements

One of the most popular ways in monetizing a blog is to sell banner ads and other ad space. You can make a lot of money with this concept alone due to the fact that they usually have a price per thousand times it's shown on the site. They are a magnet when it comes to what people look at on websites. They attract a person's interest as soon as they get on the page.

Generate Income from Your Unused Space

One of the best ways to earn income from your blog is to sell space. If your blog is generating a lot of traffic, many blog owners will be very willing to pay you a fee for putting their information in front of your readers.

Types to Avoid

Most people tend to think that flashy ads would attract others into clicking their banners, but in actuality, it keeps them from clicking. No one wants to be bothered with something flashing all the time on their screen. That makes them want to refresh the page so something non-flashing will show up. Most people are irritated by the popups and popunders and will leave a blog if there are too many. Be careful with the page peel advertisement so that they do not get in the way of your visitor every time they use the scroll bar at the top. It may be better to put them on the left side of the page instead of the right side.

Best Sizes

After concluding that you want to sell banner ads, you need to think of a size that would be best for your blog. Most people go with 125 x 125 pixels in size or 468 x 60 pixels. The best way in determining the best size is to go about resizing the banner to see if there's a noticeable change within the pixels or not. If the picture looks distorted, you'll need to resize accordingly. They should naturally fit the pages content too, so it doesn't look like it is a separate edition from the rest of your content.

Where to Place Them on the Page

The best place to put your advertisements is in the content block, as they receive the most clicks there. The left column and the header performs better than the right column and the footer area is the worst placement area.

Pricing

When it comes to selling these, most people have trouble deciding how much to charge per impression. When you are just starting out, you may want to charge roughly five dollars per thousand views. The money can add up quickly and you can be on your way to a passive income.

If you are a startup, you may encounter trouble at first when it comes to pricing the impressions for five dollars per thousand views. A great tip is to keep marketing and adding content to your blog for your impression value will go up based upon the number of visitors that you have.

OpenSky Store

OpenSky (http://www.opensky.com) is an online store that brings bloggers and suppliers together. It's free to sign up and bloggers create a profile which also serves somewhat like a store front. Bloggers can then browse through the available products and select which products they like and would appeal to their readers. Product listings display how much commission you'll make when you sell that product. In most cases, it will be a 50-50 split of the net profits on each sale.

Once a product has been added to your profile page, you'll also receive a link that can be added to your blog post, tweeted or placed on Facebook directing readers to that particular product.

Create an eBook

Many blog owners at one time or another decide to create an eBook to offer either for a price or as a free download. eBooks are a great way to expand your connection with your readers by sharing of information in an easy to read format. Most eBooks are created in a PDF format usually created in Adobe. There are some PDF creators online which will convert MS Word files to PDF however if you have affiliate hyperlinks within your document, they will not convert thus users will not be able to click on the hyperlinks. Additionally, MS Word 2010 offers a feature to save a Word document as a PDF.

Adobe offers several plans for creating PDF files online so that you're not required to purchase the software, as this can be costly. Adobe offers a free plan which provides you with 5 PDF file conversions total, 1 workspace, 3-person web conferencing, online office applications, and forum-based support. For those of us who just want to create the occasional eBook, this is a pretty good offer.

This site is very simple to use. Once you've signed up and are logged in, you simply upload your MS Word document to the workspace and then follow the on screen instructions to convert it to a PDF. Then you can simply download the PDF file to your computer.

Top Ways to Make Money with Your Blog Review

Some people blog as a hobby or just for the fun it while others hope to be able to make a some money and possibly a profit. Creating a blog that creates a cash flow requires a lot of work, patience and luck. There are a myriad of opportunities floating around on the Internet to make money with your blog.

Google AdSense

Adding Google Adsense (http://www.google.com/adsense) to your blog is simple. However, getting the most from Google AdSense is another story. Ad unit placement, size and appearance all have a direct relationship to how much you can make with AdSense . It's important to place ad units above the fold (the top half of the page), try to place ad units on the left and ad units within the body of the text work well as well.

Affiliates

As mentioned in chapter 10, signing up with affiliate groups such as Commission Junction, Linkshare and Clickbank can also result in increased earnings for your blog.

Pay per Review Sites

There are several sites in which you can enroll that will pay you to write a review for a company's product or service. I have had great success with Social Spark. View my list of product review sites in chapter 5 for more information.

The question I see most bloggers asking is how can they make money with their blogs. Many blog just for the fun it, however others would love to be able to make some cash from their passion. There are several avenues available for bloggers to monetize their blogs. Read on for more ideas.

Swagbucks

With Swag Bucks you can earn digital dollars just by searching the Internet using the Swag Bucks portal. The Swag Bucks you earn can be redeemed for Swag Bucks merchandise such as gift cards and miscellaneous merchandise.

Savvy Source

Savvy Source offers families a weekly fun filled activity. When enough people have signed up for the activity, it becomes active. Bloggers earn credit every time someone signs up and purchases the advertised activity. Credits can then be used toward activities and the Savvy Source Scholarship Fund. Savvy Source Scholarship will donate 5% of each purchase to a preschool of the purchaser's choice. They also donate 5% of each purchase to a scholarship fund created to help parents afford preschool for their children.

Product Reviews

Bloggers can sign up to give their opinions on products in return for either cash or products. Most reviews are required to be 200 words and include links to the product page. View my list of product review sites listed in chapter 5.

By utilizing one or several of these ways to make money with blogging, you will be able to build a steady stream of income online. Blogging can be a writer's dream come true. However, you must remember to be patient. It may take some time before you begin making money.

12

Three C's to Success

In this chapter, I will discuss the three C's of online communication that you need to know to build a successful business online. I am going to discuss how to make you, your message and your communication in your business more powerful. Basically, bloggers who utilize and leverage online marketing have the highest success rate. I know this because I have done it and I have had the honor of helping numerous business owners from beginners to more experienced do it too.

This chapter is about learning how to communicate more effectively and it's also about learning how to position or reposition yourself and your blog for more sales and more profits. At times, I'm sure you feel overwhelmed and frustrated. You feel as if you aren't devoting the amount of time you need to in order to stay competitive in today's marketplace.

Whether your blog offers services, sells products or you make money through advertising, these three C's to communicating online will work with all types of businesses.

When you are looking for information, entertainment or education, what is the first thing that you do? You hop on your computer and pull up Google. Why? Because content is king. All of us are looking for inspiration and education on all kinds of topics.

Whether it in the form of blogs, video, articles, product reviews, eBooks or training programs. However, it is not just about the content it is also about the connection.

We go online to connect with others and share our ideas, our articles, opinions, products or services. We also go online to connect with each other and learn more about the companies we want to do business with. And research shows that the businesses we feel the most connected to are the businesses we do repeat business with. More and more we are using the blog posts and social media to make buying decisions.

In this chapter, I'm going to share with you the three C's to online success. I'm going to go through each one and give you some tips on how to use it to increase your exposure.

#1 Connection

The first step in connecting with your audience is to identify your target market. In order to strategically grow your business, you need to know who, what and where.

The first thing you need to know is who. Who exactly is your target audience or ideal customers? Additionally, your target audience cannot be everybody. Do you want to connect with parents, seniors, business women, or small business owners?

So many entrepreneurs are not specific enough with who their market is and it is killing their business. Now I know it's really difficult to narrow it down because you don't want to leave anyone out and I understand but it's very important to identify who you are targeting. If you didn't download the target market worksheet from chapter 1, then please visit http://www.bloggingtherightway.com/downloads to grab your worksheet to help you pinpoint your target audience.

#2 Conversion

You need a website that attracts visitors and keeps them on your site longer and coming back for more. When a visitor lands on your website, you have 3 seconds to grab their attention. That's only 3 seconds! If they can't immediately know who you are and how you are going to help them, they will leave your site.

Your blog or website needs to do three main things. First, you must connect with your audience instantly. You must adequately communicate your message. Second, your blog needs to capture names and email addresses to build your list. This is so important because if you are selling products or services, the majority of visitors will not buy from you on the first visit. Figure 12.1 illustrates the number of times you typically need to follow up with a visitor before they will make a purchase from you.

If you don't setup your site to effectively to capture names and emails so you can build a relationship with them, you are missing out of potential customers. And the third thing your blog must do is convert browsers into buyers.

#3 Consistency

The last C in the plan is to be consistent. Now that you've got a blog up and running, your content and message are clear and it captures leads, it is time to add value to your audience through your communication plan. This is just a simple, strategic plan to add value to your customers on a consistent basis.

You can accomplish this through your email newsletter and other free content that you create through a blog, Facebook posts, videos, webinars or teleseminars. The key to your communication plan is to be consistent. You can't just send it out, get busy and forget for three months. Your plan should inspire, instruct and provide value to your audience.

The more you remind your audience about you and your products or services, the more likely they will want to connect with you. In fact, I have a client who calls me whenever he needs a little extra blogging help. It never fails, right after I send out my newsletter, I get a call from him requesting an appointment.

The internet is one of the most powerful business tools today. It gives you the power to connect with interesting people around the world and make an impact in people's lives. When you implement the three C's to your blogging plan, the sky's the limit.

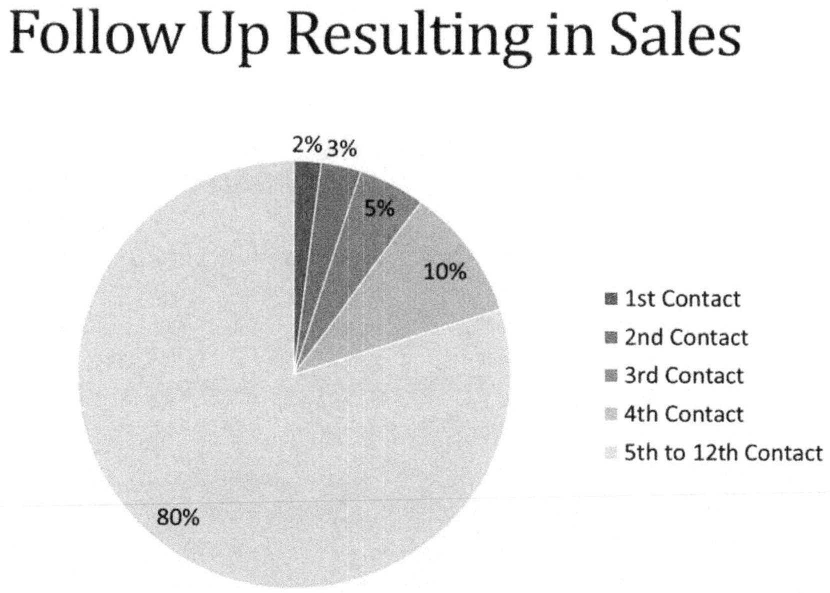

Figure 12.1 Percentage of Sales vs. Follow up

13

Develop a Blogging Plan

With how busy life is for all of us, making the most of the time we have to spend on our blogs is crucial. To help you make the most of your blogging time, I'd like to share a few of the things that I try to do on a daily basis:

Read and reply to new comments on my blog

I like to set aside at least 5 minutes to respond to *some* of the comments – as many as I can. It's important that visitors to your blog see that you are interacting with your readers so taking a few minutes each day to reply to comments needs to be part of your daily blogging ritual.

Send emails to readers who have commented on my blog

Oftentimes, readers will leave a comment on a post and then never return to read your reply. Let them know that you are answering their question and that you do appreciate them stopping by. I like to take a minute or two to visit their blog, if they have one, and then send an email letting them know that I did. In my email, I might thank them for stopping by my blog and taking the time to comment. I will also point them to other things that I have going on my blog – you will be surprised at how many re-visits you will get from sending such emails.

Check my Twitter and Facebook homepages

I like to do this to make sure there aren't any mentions of me that I need to respond to. I also like to see if there are any recent posts worth re-tweeting and sharing. Twitter and Facebook can be a big time-waster if you're not careful – I always try to limit my time on it and stick to my limits.

Glance through Google Reader

Again, this is something that I need to limit my time with. It's pretty easy to get sucked into reading posts and lose your productivity momentum. Most days, unless I'm looking for inspiration right away, I wait until all the other things on my list are done. Using Google reader is a great way to find articles to share with followers, posts to leave comments on, and inspiration for your own future posts.

Share one post or article I have found helpful

After I've looked through my reader, I try to add value to my followers by sharing at least one helpful resource I found. This is when I like to put my hashtags to good use and make my posts easy to find.

Write at least one blog post

I try to stay ahead with my posts by at least a few days. Some days, inspiration hits and I may spend a little extra time writing. Other days, I can barely crank out one post in 15 minutes. Either way, I try to spend at least 15 minutes writing. Supplying your blog with quality content is crucial to your success – it's worth being part of your daily to-do list.

Review my email

This includes replying to emails I've received and deleting emails I know that I'll never read.

Try to post a response to a forum discussion

Sharing your expertise on forums is a great way to be advertising your blog. I would recommend that you find one or two forums related to your blog and commit to visiting them regularly. Build a presence and show people that you know what you're talking about. This will encourage them to start visiting your blog to see what else you have to say.

Check my comment spam

This was just recently added to my daily list of things to do. I had never thought to do this until I randomly checked my comment spam folder one day and found several legitimate comments hidden in there! Now, I take just a minute or two to verify that the comments in the folder are actually spam and delete them right away.

Contact one other blog owner

I keep a running list of blogs that I come across that I have either enjoyed or thought that they might be interested in reading my blog. Each day, I try to contact at least one blogger on that list. Sometimes, I'm contacting them just to let them know that I appreciated a post they wrote or their blog design. It only takes a few minutes to type up an email and you never know how your words might help or encourage someone.

Scheduling Posts

As mentioned in chapter 4, posting a new blog article each day is important for your blog's success. Posting something new every day consistently brings the search engine robots to your to site which will improve your position in the search results. Additionally, having fresh material also keeps your readers interested and coming back for more. But what do you do if you're know you're going to be away from your computer or during the holidays?

Blogger and WordPress both have an option which allows users to schedule when their post will be published. This is a great tool to use if you know that you're not going to have access to your computer to keep up with your posting regimen. Additionally, some bloggers only have time to write their blog posts on the weekends. While it's not advisable to bombard your readers with five articles posted on a Saturday, scheduling these posts to go live or active on separate days helps ensure the consistency of your blog.

How it Works

Blogger

Once you have written a blog post, click "Post Options" below the text window. This will open an area with additional information. Under the "Post date and time" heading, click the "Scheduled at" radio button. Enter the date and time that you would like your post to go live. Then click "Publish".

WordPress

I use this tool in WordPress quite frequently when I have several ideas for posts and want to get them down right away before they fly right out of my head. I also recently used this tool over the Thanksgiving holiday when I knew that I was going to be out of town for several days. I knew that my blog was continuing to be updated and providing fresh information to my readers.

When you started blogging, you thought you would write daily, adding customers with each informative, witty illustration. Then, you got busy, and your blog became bi-weekly. Now you haven't written in a month, and you wonder if you are even a blogger anymore.

You are. The downside of blogging is that you are working for passive income instead of a fat advance and a deadline. When you add writer's block to the equation, you may need some help to get going again. Writers block affects everyone who writes. But what happens when you combine writer's block and burn-out? Nothing happens; all anyone hears is crickets.

Finding Time to Blog

One of the problems which many bloggers face is finding the time to blog. This is especially difficult if the blogger maintains several blogs or if the blogger maintains a current events blog in which posts must be timely in order to be relevant and of interest to the readers. Writing blog posts in batches and scheduling them to publish as needed is one way to deal with managing several blogs. However, writers of blogs related to current events must take special care to budget their time wisely to ensure they are publishing topical blog posts. One way this can be accomplished is by setting aside time daily to reading current events to derive inspiration and then scheduling time after that to write and publish the blog. For example a blogger with a current events blog might choose to review the previous day's news the first thing in the morning to ensure they are reviewing all of the relevant news from the previous day before writing the blog post.

Five tricks to help you avoid writer's block

- Schedule realistically. Daily blogging for some people is a recipe for failure. Life happens, so you need to find a more workable schedule.

- Bank a few articles. Write a lot when you are inspired but do not post your articles; instead, space them out. The WordPress "schedule" feature allows you to publish now, in a week, in a month or whenever. Use that feature.

- Buy a notebook, and look at the world like an private investigator. Notice little things, magnify them, investigate them and write them down. Take down conversations, describe people, and make a note of that weird Starbucks order. Act like a novelist and keep that notebook with you.

- Get help. You can invite guest bloggers to write or hire freelance writers to keep your blog active.

- Use apps like Evernote Web Clipper, Catch Notes, Skitch or Pocket to help you remember ideas that you run across while surfing the web.

Discouragement can take a hike. Push through blogger burn-out and get your blog back on track. Your readers will be grateful, and you will, too.

14

Tools & Resources

I am frequently asked what are the best tools for starting and maintaining a blog. My recommendations range from the best blogging platforms and hosting companies to ways to make money through advertising and affiliate marketing. Listed below are my recommendations for some useful resources to get you started with your blog, keep it going and making money.

Blogging Platforms

- WordPress.org – This is #1 recommendation, hands down! You will need to set up hosting but this will be your best choice in the long run.

- WordPress.com – Although this is free and easy to get started, you will be limited on design and functionality.

- TypePad.com

- Blogger.com - A free platform hosted by Google

Hosting

- Bluehost (http://www.bluehost.com)
- GoDaddy (http://www.godaddy.com)
- Host Gator (http://www.hostgator.com)

Themes

- Themeforest (http://www.themeforest.net)
- Woothemes (http://www.woothemes.com)
- StudioPress (http://www.studiopress.com)

Training

- Learn How to Blog Today (http://www.learnhowtoblogtoday.com)
- Blogging with John Chow (http://www.bloggingwithjohnchow.com)

Monetization

- AdSense (http://www.google.com/adsense)
- Chitika (http://www.chitika.com)
- Shopzilla (http://www.shopzilla.com)
- Amazon (https://affiliate-program.amazon.com)

Tools

- Feedburner (http://www.feedburner.com)
- Aweber (http://www.aweber.com)
- Vertical Response (http://www.verticalresponse.com)
- HootSuite (http://www.hootsuite.com)
- Google Analytics (http://www.google.com/analytics)
- Google Reader (http://www.google.com/reader)
- Akismet (http://www.akismet.com)
- Mail Chimp (http://www.mailchimp.com)
- Constant Contact (http://www.constantcontact.com)
- Adrive (http://www.adrive.com)
- Google Documents (http://www.google.com/docs)
- Google Voice (http://www.google.com/voice)
- Gravity Forms (http://www.gravityforms.com)

Google Docs

Google Docs or Google Documents (http://www.google.com/docs) in a free online application offered by Google which allows users to create or upload documents, spreadsheets, presentations, forms and drawings. These documents can be edited, shared or embedded into web pages.

Google Docs form feature is a quick and easy way to create forms within your blog or website. Users create the form within Google Docs and then embed a small line of code into the page or post. When a visitor fills out the form, the information automatically is added to a spreadsheet within Google Documents. You can set up a notification for Google Docs to send you an email whenever a new entry has been added to this spreadsheet.

To get started using Google Docs, you simply visit http://www.google.com/documents and create a Google account if you don't already have a one. Then click "Create new" from the drop down menu on the left and then choose "Form". This is a very simple tool to use and I definitely recommend using it if you want to have a form on your blog or website.

MyContactForm.com

MyContactForm.com is a free online service that walks users step by step through the process of creating online forms. Online forms can be used to collect information such as personal, subscription, job listings, etc.

MyContactForm.com has a wizard that allows you to design forms with as many fields as you want. Users can also specify where the data collected is to be emailed. The site is free to sign up and create forms. After using the wizard to create the form and create the HTML, the user then simply copies the code and places it on their website.

Docstoc

Docstoc (http://www.docstoc.com) is an online service where bloggers can store, share, sell and find documents. Docstoc also provides technology which allows users to embed documents right into their webpage or blog post. This technology also allows readers the option of reading the document online or downloading it to their computer.

Docstoc also gives users the option to sell their documents with no upfront or recurring fees for the first 60 days and sellers keep 100% of all sales. After 60 days, the proceeds from all sales are split evenly between the seller and Docstoc (sellers keep 50% of all sales). Payments are issued within 30 days of the last day of each month once your balance reaches $100.

Users can also make money through Google AdSense displayed alongside documents which have been made public on Docstocs.

Blog and Website owners who have eBooks can make them available to users by uploading a copy of the eBook on their site. Users can scroll through the eBook or download it to their computers.

If you have an eBook you would like sell or provide to your readers, visit Docstocs to learn more about the services they offer.

Hootsuite

If you are new to the online space and want to learn internet marketing there are a lot of different concepts that are accessible to attract traffic for your internet marketing products. One of these utilizes the power of many popular social networking websites and in turn gives your internet marketing products exposure.

HootSuite (http://www.hootsuite.com) is a great tool to automate the system that is social networking.

You can probably relate, I recall the time I first began to learn about the many social networking sites online from twitter to foursquare I began to feel overwhelmed. Not by the amount of the social networking sites but instead the time required to be spent in order to make use of the main ones. To market on Twitter alone seemed like a forty hour job not to mention LinkedIn. As a result of being very overwhelmed, I avoided the social networking side of things for a very long time.

I did not visit the social sites for anything other than my own personal entertainment, until one day I was spending some time on an online forum and I read up about this tool named HootSuite. The forum member said that he was able to run all of the major social network sites through HootSuite and it only was taking him a day each month to get his social networking activity out of the way. I found this tricky to believe, but out of curiosity I decided to sign up for HootSuite and began looking around at what it could do.

HootSuite is an excellent social management tool that literally handles all the social networking you could think of.

You can sign up for LinkedIn, Twitter, Facebook profiles, Facebook pages, Foursquare, Ping.fm, MySpace and WordPress just to name a few. HootSuite allows you to make status updates on each of the social networking sites at once. So if I was to say I am hungry, bring me food and then chose to send to all networks, HootSuite within no time would automatically send out the update across my networks for all of my friends to see.

HootSuite also has another valuable feature that is priceless if you are really busy. HootSuite lets you schedule updates, days, months or even years ahead of time. All you need to have is a day to invest submitting updates to a file to upload and HootSuite will sort out the rest.

This element means that you do not ever again have to sit in front of the computer all day submitting updates because HootSuite will sort out everything for you.

HootSuite is definitely the ideal tool for anyone who is looking for mass exposure.

Networked Blogs

Wondering how you to automatically submit your blog posts to Facebook? A lot of people use Hootsuite to syndicate their RSS feeds to their social media channels. Using Hootsuite is a great tool however I have noticed that when Hootsuite brings in the blog posts, at times it leaves off the picture associated with the post.

Having the picture along with the post in Facebook is extremely important to me as 80% of users will click on a Facebook post with a picture over other types of content.

There is a good solution right within Facebook. It's an app called Networkedblogs (http://www.networkedblogs.com). It is also pretty simple to set up. Here's how:

- Locate the app at http://www.networkedblogs.com.
- Click on "Register a Blog".
- Add your blog's URL or website address and click "Next".
- Complete the form with information about your blog and click "Next".
- You will be asked to verify that you are the owner of the blog.

- After ownership is verified, you can choose the social media channels (i.e., Facebook or Twitter) that you would like to link your blog to.

- Once you confirm this syndication, your all set.

Additionally, you can choose multiple Facebook Page or Twitter Profiles. This is a great tool to ensure that your followers are keeping up with your latest news.

Ghost Writers

For a company's blog, there may come a time when they need help keeping their blog active and maintained. A good option for them is to hire a ghost writer. A ghost writer can create the content of the blog post touching on the main points. Once the ghost writer has started the post, the business owner can come in and add their personal touches.

In my experience, I have found that business owners aren't sure what to blog about or how to get started. This is a where a ghost writer or blog writing company can help out.

My company, CB Virtual Services (http://www.cbvirtualservices .com), does just that. We design a blogging strategy, prepare the editorial calendar and then create the blog posts. We also provide our blog structure expertise to ensure that the business receives the most impact from each post.

Cool Webmaster Tools

Managing your site and creating a new blog becomes easier these days with lots of online tools than can help you all throughout the process. Here are some little known but cool webmaster tools that you may want to explore:

- Copyscape (http://www.copyscape.com) is an online tool that allows you to search for copies of your page on the web. It can also protect you from cases of plagiarism. You can defend your sites with a free plagiarism warning banner from Copyscape. While this is a free service, there is also the Copyscape Premium that provides more powerful plagiarism detection. There are also additional features such as copy-paste originality checks, batch search, private index, case tracking and an API.

- PickyDomains (http://www.pickydomains.com). When you are thinking of setting up a new website, there are many tools you can use to get started. First of all, you have to think of an effective and unique domain name. As what most people say, you must keep it short and simple (KISS). But if you are out of ideas, you can use PickyDomains to come up with great domain names. It's a risk free naming service that when you need a domain and you can't think of one, so you just have to place your order and you pay only if you receive suggestions you like.

- iSpionage (http://www.ispionage.com) is a reliable tool in managing client campaigns, analyzing SEO results, monitoring affiliates and more. It can be used for free and you can enter any site to learn which keywords generate traffic for them especially if they spend money on pay-per-click (PPC).

  It is a search marketing tool that can also guide you in starting up your online business. It is popular tool used in keyword monitoring, keyword research and building campaigns.

- BannerFans (http://www.bannerfans.com) is a free online banner-maker that webmasters can take advantage of. Banners have many uses and most websites use it to promote the webpages, products or services. Webmasters also incorporate the site identity on it. There are different sizes of banners and if you want to make use of predefined sizes as well as experience hassle-free banner making, then BannerFans is good for you. It is very easy to use. You can use it to generate blog headers, text banners, large buttons and many others. You don't need to be an expert with Photoshop and other editing software to come up with cool banners. With BannerFans, everything will be easier!

- FreeLogoServices (http://www.freelogoservices.com). Aside from banners, website logos are also important. People can easily identify you with your logo so it is essential to come up with unique and relevant design. Creating a logo with FreeLogoServices is easy and fast. You just enter the logo text, choose a design, customize your logo, then save and download. FreeLogoServices is a trusted online tool because of the quality output and large selection of designs. You can try it for free and make a logo design in few minutes!

- Alexa.com (http://www.Alexa.com) is an online tool used to analyze site's performance and other statistics. It shows if the site is popular or not and lists all similar sites, which is very handy, and very useful if you are planning to launch a new site in the existing niche.

  If your site is 3 months or older, you can also view its online analytics through Alexa. There are site tools and site info that you can check to know more about your website. You can even compare it to your competitors. What's more, you can download and install Alexa toolbar for Google Chrome to easily monitor traffic rank, see related links, view search analytics and read website reviews.

- Broken Link Check (http://www.brokenlinkcheck.com). Backlinks are important to webmasters. This is why a particular broken link can cost much trouble and adverse impact on site traffic. To avoid this issue, it would be better to use Broken Links Tool which is an easy and quick-to-use online tool in checking broken or dead links. You can choose what type of links you would like to check – inbound links, outbound links or both (all links).

How to Create a Grab Buttons

What is a grab button? A grab button is a 125 x 125 pixel graphic which personal niche bloggers can copy the code of and add it to their blogs to advertise your blog. Additionally, you can do the same of other blogs that are in your niche. A grab button can be a photograph of you, your family or anything else that interests you. It can also be a clipart graphic.

Step 1

If you want to use a clipart graphic, then the first step is to find a graphic that suits you and/or your blog. There are many free clipart sites where you can find the right graphic.

- Once you've decided on a photograph or graphic, open an image editing application to a new project.

- Upload your graphic into the new project.

- If you want, you can change the background color and add any additional features.

Another option is to use a cropped version of your blog header.

- Open your blog in a browser window.
- Push the "Print Screen" button on your keyboard.
- Open an image editing application and choose a new project.
- Paste (ctrl + v) onto the new project.
- Crop the area of this graphic that you want to use for your button. (Don't worry about the size at this time).

Step 2

Add text on top of the picture, clipart or graphic choosing which font you like. Preferably this is the blog's title. Save a copy to your computer as a backup.

Step 3

On the image editing application's toolbar, find the option to "resize image". Set the new size of the image to 125 x 125 pixels.

Step 4

If the image looks good, then save it to your computer. If not, go back to Step 2 and make changes.

Step 5

Upload your grab button to your hosting domain file manager or Photobucket (for example).

Step 6

Add the button with code to your blog sidebar so that others can easily grab it.

Step 7

Your button should now look something like this.

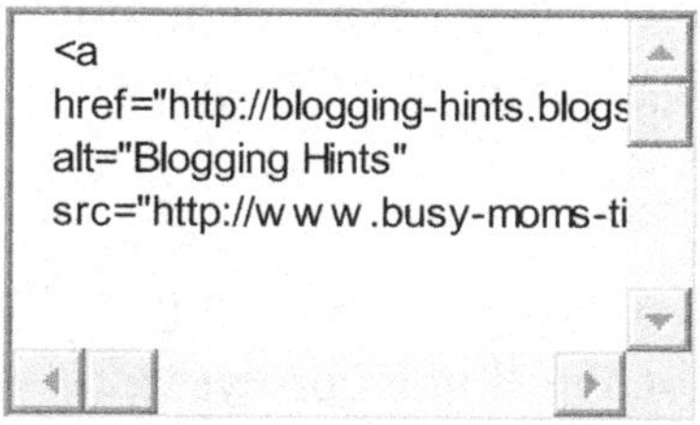

Image Editing Tools

At one time or another you may need to create and edit photographs and images. The computer you are using may not have image editing software installed on it. I have discovered a few online imaging tools which do the job quite nicely.

- Lunapic (http://www131.lunapic.com/editor)
- Splashup (http://www.splashup.com)

How to Create a Scrolling Blog Roll

The longer we blog the more buttons and links we acquire. Displaying these buttons and links without cluttering your blog pages and sidebars can be tricky. A good way to display all of your buttons and links without cluttering your sidebar is to create a scrolling blog roll. This method simply uses the html marquee code. Listed below is the code to create your own upward scrolling blog roll. Replace the code in purple with a blog's button code.

```
< marquee onmouseover="this.stop()" direction="up"
onmouseout="this.start()" scrollamount="4" loop="true" width="180"
height="230" > < a href="http://www.blog-address.com/" > < img
border="0" alt="Blog Name" src="http://www.blog-button.jpg" / >
< /a > < /marquee >
```

*Note: There is a bug when viewing with Internet Explorer. Sometimes it will not scroll in IE browser.

Create a Favicon

A Favicon (short for favorite icon) is the small icon on the browser address bar. Having your own Favicon adds professionalism to your blog or website. Here are the steps to creating your own Favicon.

1. Visit http://www.favicongenerator.com/ to create or your own Favicon.

2. Browse for the image on your computer that you would like to use as your Favicon. If you've already created a button, you can select that to use as your Favicon.

3. Click "Generate Favicon".

4. Save your newly created Favicon as "favicon.ico".

5. Upload your new Favicon to your root directory, Photobucket or directory where you store your blog's images.

6. Add the following code to the section of your blog template or website replacing "/favicon.icon" with the correct path to your Favicon:

   < link href='/favicon.ico' rel='shortcut icon'/ >
   < link href='favicon.ico' rel='icon'/ >

That's all there is to it. If you have any questions, please contact me and I'll be more than happy to help.

Installing a Favicon in WordPress

If there is already an old favicon.ico file in your current theme's main folder, you will need to delete it using FTP Clients.

1. With an FTP Client, upload the new favicon.ico file into your current theme's main folder.

2. Upload another copy of your favicon.ico file to the main directory of your site (ie. http://example.com/favicon.ico).

This will display the favicon in your subscribers' feedreaders.

3. In order for your favicon to show up in some older browsers, you will need to edit your page header.

4. Go to your WordPress Administration Panel.

5. Click on Design (called Presentation in WordPress 2.3.x and below, and Appearance in WordPress 2.7+).

6. Click on Theme Editor.

7. Select the file called Header or header.php to edit the file.

8. Search for the line of code that begins with

<link rel="shortcut icon" and ends with /favicon.ico" />. Overwrite it, if it exists, or add the following code below the <head> HTML tag.

<link rel="shortcut icon" href="<?php echo get_stylesheet_directory_uri(); ?>/favicon.ico" />

9. Save the changes.

Source: WordPress.org.

15

Take it to the Next Level

Believe it or not a lot of people start blogging as a way to make money online then give it a couple of months and quit. Rather than quit there may be some alternatives. First, I would like to state that a couple of months is not a long enough time to find out if your model would be a success. Think of it as a business and give it a year. Now on to my subject, I will tell you how to take those skills you have learned from blogging and turn them into real money.

When you start, you will learn a few of things such as on and off page SEO, link building, content creation, website design, ad placement, social networking and content management systems just to name a few. All of those can be turned in to freelance or real jobs and in combination with the co-operation with the bloggers you have met and mingle with daily you could expand your operation. After a year of blogging, you will have a knowledge about the internet that most people or companies on the net do not.

Perhaps you have a large following of people that read your blog and love it. Your passion excited them. Take what you know about content creation and pair with a web designer, fellow blogger and post ads on craigslist stating that you will write articles. You can get paid just for writing unique articles for people. Also web designers need writers for websites that they are setting up, sometimes the designer and owner of the site do not want to write the content.

Perhaps you have 1,500 fans on Facebook and 3,000 followers on twitter. You could be the next social media guru, market yourself and look for someone that needs a social media guru. Companies trying to expand or startup on the internet will hire people to run their social media campaign once they find out how involved it is. You can scour Craigslist or contact web Designers and a lot of them outsource the social media campaigns of their clients.

Did you create a great looking blog? You might be ready to step up to web design, you could do themes, psd's, logo's or any other number of items, start to network with designers and you can get started by just creating some small items for them or creating a bloggers logo, work on building a portfolio and then you will be able to present it to people to get work.

If you were good at all of these and just want to expand then you could pair with people to build your client base and in the meantime start a website selling your services. I have created one with all of the services that I offer so that when I discuss with people what I can do they can view it visually also. Whatever the case, take what you have learned and find someone who needs that service. Simple as that, oh, and don't give up….

The Financial and Personal Benefits of Career Blogging

There are many benefits to pursuing a career in blogging. Perhaps one of the most alluring benefits to a career in blogging is the work can typically be done as a telecommute position. This is because as long as the blogger has access to a pc and the software necessary to write and upload a blog, there is no need for the blogger to perform the work from any specific location. This means the blogger can live virtually anywhere in the world and can probably perform the necessary work from his own home. However, not all career blogging positions are telecommute positions. Some organizations may prefer their bloggers to perform the work on-site as a matter of company policy.

Another benefit to a career in blogging is the ability to accomplish work at a pace which is convenient to the blogger. The blogger is usually required to upload a new post to the blog according to a regular schedule but the actual writing of the posts can be accomplished when it is convenient for the blogger. As previously discussed, many blogging software packages enable the blogger to set a specific time for a specific post to be uploaded. This allows the blogger to write several posts at a time and have them published according to a pre-determined schedule.

You're a Professional

You're a professional now! What are you still doing with that free blog hosting service? It is time to upgrade to a domain hosted solution. You need to get a web host and choose a domain name for your blog then check its availability. Select the blogging software you wish to use, such as WordPress.org. When you have your new blog domain setup and ready for traffic then it is time for you to announce your move on all your previous blog accounts.

Your last entry to the blog should be a "move" announcement. The title should be "Moved" and the blog entry should state something like "Old Blog has been moved to New Blog please follow and bookmark this link for future reference". This way all returning visitors and new readers should not have any problem finding your new blog domain.

At the level of a professional blogger you may want to team up with 1 or more other bloggers. This will create a more interesting and more powerful blog. The old saying "two heads are better than one", more authors mean more advertising and exposure because each author will have a vested interest in the blog. The idea of a team blog is to make it profitable and rewarding for all authors, while continuing to target the blog topic and keeping the blog interesting for visitors.

Following these blogging techniques should make your blogging experience much more rewarding. There is no guarantee that your blog will become popular or a household name, but the effort should at least put you one step closer. Making money online is not an overnight experience like many may think, but making money online is definitely a foreseeable possibility. As well, growing popularity on the web is not an overnight experience, but through time, dedication, and persistence you will be rewarded with all the royalties of blogging.

The Future Looks Bright for Mom Bloggers

In Jennifer James' article, "Why Top Mom Bloggers Have Greater Earning Power" she discusses how mom bloggers are leaving their marks on the blogging community. I just read a recent study that showed that Mom bloggers are filling a niche and filling it well. In fact, Mom bloggers are expected to see earnings growth within the next few years.

James further explains how brands are also recognizing these bloggers and how they are having a tremendous impact. From my own personal experience, I was surprised at how many Mom (and Dad) related blogs were out there on the Internet. With so many to choose from, this opens up a whole new marketing avenue for brand companies. Why not have the very people who use their product, review it and give their opinions to other Moms who use their products.

I'm excited to be a part of this growing trend of Mommy bloggers and I hope I can be a contributing member of this niche. Blogging is a constant learning process. I learn something new every day and I try and pass it along to my readers. So keep up the good work fellow Mommy bloggers – they have their eyes on us.

Book Publishing

For some bloggers an obvious next step from being a blog writer is to become an author. Some bloggers start out by publishing eBooks with the next step being publication of a book for sale in retail outlets.

Additionally, many authors are going the self-publishing route as well. What is great about writing a blog is that all of those daily or weekly blog posts can be transformed into a book. Providing readers with value through books is a great way to increase your audience as well as open doors to new opportunities.

Speaking Engagements

If you stick with blogging long enough and then eventually move to being an author, often times speaking opportunities start popping up. For some people, this is a scary and uncomfortable thought. Yet other people can't wait to get in front of an audience and share their information.

Some of my friends and family are surprised that I love speaking as much as I do. I am quiet natured and soft spoken so it is assumed that I wouldn't feel comfortable in front of a room of people. But it is quite the opposite.

Keep your eyes open for opportunities to share your information and knowledge with others. Before you know it, you may be speaking all across the U.S.

16

Blogging Success Stories

As I started on my blogging journey, there were many people along the way who inspired, instructed and motived me. In this chapter, I would like to share with you the influential people who made a difference in my blogging career.

Darren Rowse

Darren Rowse is a full time blogger and owner of ProBlogger.net (http://www.problogger.net), Digital Photography School (http://www.digital-photography-school.com/blog), FeelGooder (http://www.feelgooder.com) and TwiTip (http://www.twitip.com/). Darren states, "In 2002, I stumbled upon an article about 'Blogging'. I didn't know it at the time but that moment changed my life."

Shortly after reading that article, Darren started a personal blog (http://www.livingroom.org.au/blog) where he explored issues of Pop Culture, Spirituality and Blogging.

Over time, his blogs grew from a hobby to a part-time job and now a he is a full-time blogger influencing thousands of fellow bloggers on a daily basis.

Darren Rowse was my inspiration when I started blogging. His book, "Problogger – Secrets for Blogging your Way to a Six-Figure Income" provided me with the tools I needed to get started and become a successful blogger.

John Chow

John Chow (http://www.johnchow.com) is a blogger, speaker and entrepreneur. Within a period of two years, John was able to take his blog from making $0 to over $40,000 a month.

JohnChow.com is one of the leading blogs online with thousands of daily readers and followers. John's blog provides information on internet marketing and how to make money online.

John's website provides me with valuable tools and resources that I utilize on a consistent basis.

Julie and Julia

"Julie & Julia" is a 2009 movie written and directed by Nora Ephron. The movie stars Meryl Streep, Stanley Tucci, Amy Adams, and Chris Messina. The film is about a young woman, Julie Powell, who desires to cook all 524 recipes in Julia Child's cookbook in 365 days. Julie, the main character, shares her experience on her blog which eventually leads to the opportunity for her to become a published author.

Ephron's screenplay is adapted from "My Life in France", Child's autobiography written with Alex Prud'homme, and a memoir by Julie Powell documenting online her daily experiences cooking each of the 524 recipes in Child's "Mastering the Art of French

Cooking". This was the first major motion picture to be based on a blog.

This was the movie that inspired me to become a blogger. Within days of seeing this movie, I made the decision to start my first blog and I have never looked back. And similarly to Julie Powell, I too am now a published author – all thanks to a blog.

Ree Drummond

Ree Drummond is also known as the Pioneer Woman (http://thepioneerwoman.com). Her enormously popular blog shares her life as a ranch wife and mother of four.

Ree is also a published author of several books including "The Pioneer Woman Cooks" and "Charlie the Ranch Dog".

She is also the host of "The Pioneer Woman" on The Food Network where she prepares down home recipes.

Ree's blog is entertaining and engaging. From the moment I came across her highly successful blog, I wanted to emulate her. I wanted my blog to be just as inviting and entertaining as hers.

17

Final Thoughts

Blogging is no longer just a hobby. It has become a powerful marketing tool and I'm excited to be a part of its evolution.

I'm passionate about blogging because of the opportunities that are made available to those who appreciate and harness its power.

Writing a blog allows people to share their passions, their challenges and their accomplishments. It also gives them a way to entertain, enrich, and educate.

A blog can boost a company's sales or provide the stay-at-home mom with the ability to earn some extra money while taking care of the children.

It is my passion and I'm proud to call myself a blogger.

Acknowledgements

This book would not have been possible without the support and encouragement of my husband, Chris Buccieri.

For understanding my long nights at the computer and helping me create the title of this book, I'd like to thank my children, Michael and Alyssa.

Words cannot express my gratitude to Audra Erwin, The High on Life Coach, for her professional advice, assistance and support in publishing this book.

Thank you to Dagmar Gatell for contributing your SEO expertise to this book and being such a great friend and business partner.

Jessica Brace, thank you for contributing such great information on video marketing to this book.

To Christina Stuart, thank you for the beautiful picture you took of me. You definitely capture a person's essence.

Logo Nerds (http://www.logonerds.com), thank you helping put the finishing touches on my book cover.

Lisa Palmer, thank you for your assistance throughout the marketing process and helping me remain organized.

Thank you to the Women's Prosperity Network (WPN) founding sisters, Nancy Matthews, Trish Carr and Susan Wiener, for your resources and guidance.

Last but not least I would like to thank my parents, Ed and Lee Ward, for their continued support in all of my endeavors.

About the Author

As a Speaker, Author, Web Designer, and Blogger Cindy Buccieri combines her 20 years of Internet savvy and desire to help others with her intuitive understanding of technology. She engages and enlightens audiences while providing easy to understand solutions to their blogging and online challenges.

Cindy Buccieri is the owner of CB Virtual Services (http://www.cbvirtualservices.com), an internet marketing and Web design company committed to helping others achieve success in their business. Cindy is also a blogging expert and Internet consultant providing information and insights to those who want to learn about these cutting edge marketing techniques to further the success of their business.

Cindy possesses a Bachelor of Science degree in Information Studies and has worked for Fortune 500 companies such as McDonnell Douglas and Northrop Grumman. She also freelanced as a web designer, blogger and internet marketer for several years. In 2009, Cindy launched Busy Mom's Tips, a blog which provides helpful tips for today's busy moms. Three additional blogs launched shortly thereafter. The creation and marketing of these blogs provided her with first-hand experience into what is takes to increase traffic to a blog, develop a following and make money from it.

Cindy is also the author of several eBooks including, "Busy Mom's Ultimate Guide to Finding the Perfect Work at Home Job", "How to Increase Traffic to Your Blog", and"Launch Your Blog in 7 Days". She also has several articles published on Associated Content, Hubpages and eHow.

While Cindy has experience in many areas of business including Internet marketing and Web development, her passion is in Blogging. Additionally, Cindy loves being able to share with others her knowledge on this vast subject through speaking and consulting.

Cindy's Most Popular Presentation Topics

The 3 Keys to Internet Marketing Success

Are you overwhelmed trying to market your business online? Stop spinning your wheels and learn the 3 keys to having a successful online business. In this presentation Cindy reveals the 3 keys that will allow you to harness the power of the Internet to engage customers, increase your profits and drive a flood of traffic to your website.

Build It and They Will Come: Steps to Creating a Successful Website.

Discover why the "Build it and They Will Come" philosophy does not work in the online Field of Dreams. In this presentation, Cindy reveals how to design a website that is attractive to search engines which will drive qualified prospects to your site that you can then convert into buyers. This presentation also covers why building your contact list is vital to your business success and provides easy and affordable systems to build it now.

Why Having a Blog is Not an Option…It's a Necessity!

Learn why a blog is important to your online success as well as how to write the perfect blog post to drive traffic and engage readers. This presentation also addresses the misconception about a blog's purpose, location, keywords and topics.

Communicating with Your Audience: Know the 3 C's

Discover the 3 C's of online communication: Consistency, Connection and Conversion. This presentation discusses how important it is to consistently connect with your audience and how to convert your audience from browsers to buyers.

To learn how Cindy can help you take your blog to the next level, visit her online at CindyBuccieri.com

About the Author

Index

Made in the USA
Monee, IL
04 November 2026

67386999R00108